DON'T WORRY ABOUT IT

Don't Worry About It: Go to Bed

Copyright © 2023 Keith Banks-Obanor. All rights reserved.

No rights claimed for public domain material, all rights reserved. No parts of this publication may be reproduced, stored in any retrieval system, or transmitted in any form or by any means, electronic, mechanical, recording, or otherwise, without the prior written permission of the author. Violations may be subject to civil or criminal penalties.

Unless stated otherwise, all Scriptures are taken from the King James Version of the Holy Bible.

ISBN: 979-8-9893276-0-7 (hardback)
        979-8-9893276-1-4 (paperback)

Aspire Publications

Printed in United States of America

DON'T WORRY ABOUT IT

GO TO BED

*This book is going to unlock
your willpower to overcome worry,
fear, and anxiety.*

KEITH BANKS-OBANOR

Foreword by Bishop Dr. Gideon A. Thompson

TABLE OF CONTENTS

FOREWORD BY BISHOP GIDEON A. THOMPSON 7

DEDICATION 9

RECOMMENDATION—WHAT OTHERS ARE SAYING. 11

ACKNOWLEDGMENT AND APPRECIATION 15

ABOUT THE AUTHOR 17

INTRODUCTION 19

CHAPTER ONE: YOU ARE NOT WIRED
    FOR A LIFE OF WORRY 27

CHAPTER TWO: 12 WAYS THAT LIFE
    GETS YOU TO WORRY 39

CHAPTER THREE: FAITH OVER FEAR 49

CHAPTER FOUR: IT IS ALL IN YOUR HEAD 61

CHAPTER FIVE: THE MEDICAL, PSYCHOLOGICAL
    & EMOTIONAL EFFECTS OF FEAR,
    WORRY & ANXIETY 73

CHAPTER SIX: THE LIES THAT WORRY PRODUCES 81

CHAPTER SEVEN: THE ANTIDOTE |
    CURE FOR WORRY 87

CHAPTER EIGHT: THE KEYS TO A RESTFUL SLEEP 97

CHAPTER NINE: TOOLS FOR OVERCOMING
    WORRY, FEAR & ANXIETY 103

CHAPTER TEN: THE 10 BASIC NEEDS THAT WE WORRY
   ABOUT THE MOST 109
CHAPTER ELEVEN: GO TO BED. IT WILL BE ALL
   OVER IN THE MORNING 113

FOREWORD BY BISHOP GIDEON A. THOMPSON

This new book by Keith Banks-Obanor is a refreshing look at the insightful ministry truths taught in Scripture. The author, a pioneer pastor of a growing local church in Boston, the largest metropolitan city in New England, has opened the windows of his church experiences to share the truth that is desperately needed but still unknown in many circles.

Keith Banks-Obanor is a cutting-edge, charismatic leader who is filled and led by the power of the Holy Spirit. By recognizing the inherent difficulties of inner-city life, he has wisely structured his ministry to respond to the personal challenges that create spiritual, economic, and relational struggles with Black and White inner-city dwellers. Having a solid foundation in spiritual, biblical truth has served to equip this man of God and his wife and family with the tools they have successfully used to establish avenues of salvation and deliverance in the lives of their congregants.

Pastor Keith and his wife have lived and practiced the simple truths taught in the Scriptures for years. God the Father has called this godly couple to "Go make disciples of all peoples, through the ministry process of baptizing and teaching them," as a result, the Lord has blessed and strengthened their local church. It is not uncommon to hear the testimonies of those who are part of their ministry spoken in terms of the benefits of healing and deliverance: congregants who, through faith, have experienced Abundant Life in

Christ and who, through their ministry connections, are now strong, Spirit-filled believers who God is using to touch their local world with the good news of salvation in Christ.

I've known Pastor Keith and his wife for several decades and found them to be the real deal when walking and living as genuine believers. They love each other and are deeply committed to the truths of God's Word. They both walk in full fellowship with believers of precious faith, and as disciples of Christ, they are determined to make a difference in their world.

As Keith's bishop and spiritual father oversees his ministry and occasionally preaches for him, I love him dearly and recommend this powerful book. Its truth will certainly be a source of blessing and inspiration to you.

Respectfully submitted,

Bishop Dr. Gideon A. Thompson,
Jubilee Christian Church (JCC),
JCC: 1500 Blue Hill Ave, Boston, Ma.
JCC: 1278 Park St, Stoughton, MA. JCC:
JCC: at Holden Chapel, 279 Reservoir St., Holden, MA 01520

DEDICATION

I would like to dedicate this project, first to my "TeamBanks" - the love of my life and my queen, Sogie Banks; my firstborn and my everything, Charisma Banks; my heart and my angel, Sharon Banks; and my buddy, my one and only loving son, Joey Banks. They are my greatest supporters and my inspiration. They are the reason why I thrive and aspire for more.

To the loving memory of my grandmother, Grandma Mary Omobusi. Grandma took me in along with her when she went to live with her oldest son, my uncle, Chief DU Edebiri, in the late '70s. I was only 7 years old. Grandma taught me how to cook, clean, and take care of the space that we all shared. She taught me some valuable lessons that have shaped me into the man I am today, especially since I didn't grow up with both of my biological parents. Despite my family background and dysfunctions, I have always wanted to raise a great family of my own, be successful, and become someone that others can look up to someday.

As a teenager, I can still remember telling Grandma Mary some of the dreams I had while sleeping. I told Grandma that in my dreams, I was always with a group of white folks, working with them in big companies. Grandma simply gave me her interpretation by saying, "Son, your destiny is not in this part of the world (Africa)." She said that someday I was going to end up in a foreign land, and it never occurred to me then that my destiny was in America.

So fast forward, after many decades since Grandma has gone home to be with her ancestors, here I am, living and fulfilling my dream in accordance with the interpretation, foresight, and profound wisdom given by Grandma.

I have written and published two great books in the U.S., raised a great family that loves and supports me and my ministry - a loving wife, and three great children that we have put through college. We have also planted a great church and started a couple of businesses. To God be the glory!

And lastly, to the loving memory of my uncle, Chief Dr. D.U. Edebiri, the Esogban of Benin Kingdom, Edo State, Nigeria, who transitioned to eternal peace on July 20th, 2023. His transition happened while the manuscript of this book was already sent to my publisher, and in progress of being published . So, I had to put a pause to the publishing process so that I could write a short dedication to his memory. "The Boss," which was the nickname for my late uncle, was the man who opened his home to me after my biological father abandoned me. He became the father figure in my life. He paid my way through primary and high school. He was a brave, resilient, influential, and industrious man. In the 13 years that I lived with him, his resilience, relentlessness, and bravery rubbed off on me, shaping me to become the man I am today.

Farewell, big boss. Rest in peace, Daddy. I am eternally grateful for your influence upon my life.

RECOMMENDATION—WHAT OTHERS ARE SAYING.

Don't Worry About It: Go to Bed

Worry is the proof you are convinced that your problem or issue is unsolvable. Worry is confidence in your crisis. No one can win when their mind and feelings are in a position of worry. When we stress, we lose sleep, creativity, and valuable moments. If you can't master your mind, you won't be able to master your feelings… which eventually will lead to loss of incredible time and [lack of] great success. A thought that lasts for more than 30 seconds turns into a feeling. [So] instead of conquering a thought, you must now fight a feeling and a thought. In Keith Banks-Obanor's newest book, *Don't Worry About It: Go To Bed*, you will discover the key to life's greatest secret: How to trust and overcome deadly emotions.

Dr. Jerry A. Grillo
Presiding Bishop Church One

* * *

In our world, there are great preachers, pastors, writers, and leaders, but every now and then, we are graced with truth ambassadors who have paved a road with their lives. With the stroke of his pen, my brother, Pastor Keith Banks-Obanor, has downloaded a blueprint to the world to teach us how to live a life free of worry, anxiety, and stress… To God Be All the Glory!!!

Pastor Matthew K. Thompson
Senior Pastor
Jubilee Christian Church—Boston, Stoughton, Worcester, Ma

**

I am extremely honored to recommend Pastor Keith's newest, must-read book, "Don't Worry About It…Go to bed. We live in a day when fear, worry, and anxiety attempt to control our emotions, drain us of our energy, and cloud our decision-making. Pastor Keith gives us the tools, equips us to combat the weapons of our soul, and guides us into how we can live a worry-free, victorious, peaceful life."

Evangelist Debra George
Dr. Rod Parsley's ministry Evangelist www.DebraGeorge.org

**

I am honored to endorse Pastor Keith's amazing book, "Don't Worry About It…Go to bed. What a great reminder that we are not wired to worry. I've learned in my personal life that worrying can affect not only your mental health but also your physical health. Pastor Keith is practical in equipping us with the knowledge of how worrying affects us and giving us the tools to fight against it. I highly recommend this book!

Phil Thompson
Gospel Recording Artist

BOOKS BY KEITH BANKS-OBANOR

YOUR DAILY DEVOTIONAL BOOK

ACKNOWLEDGMENT AND APPRECIATION

It was about 9 years ago… 2014… to be precise. With a bible in one hand, a microphone, and a pillow in the other hand… I introduced a message of hope to our Congregation… titled… "Don't worry about it…Go to bed." It was a message that examined how worry, anxiety, and fear… impact our mental health and overall wellbeing. The response was tremendous… I saw a need for such knowledge and remedy… that could help people overcome… and live a healthier and victorious life. So right then and there… I told our congregation that the message title would be a Book… my heart believed it… my spirit incubated it for 9 whole years… writing manuscripts and gathering resources… and the rest, they say, is history.

This project would have been impossible for me without the generous sponsorship of Boston's self-made billionaire, philanthropist, and founder of the Herb chambers group of companies… Mr Herbert G Chambers. Herb, I am eternally grateful to God for your place in my life and ministry. You sponsored my first book… and again single-handedly sponsored this one. Your support for my ministry over the years is unequivocally enormous. You are indeed my hero. I am the man I am today because of your influence in my life… May God give you many more years to thrive.

To my amazing team-Banks! My Besties:

First... to my lovely Queen(Sogie), the mother of my incredible 3... thanks for your support over the years. You came into my life when I had nothing... you are highly appreciated for sticking with me through every grind and storm. Love you to the moon and back

To my incredible 3...Charisma, Sharon, and Jeoy. You are why I can't stop, won't stop, and can't quit. My most significant investment and legacy is putting all three of you through college. Pops loves y'all so dearly. Find your place in this world and be a world changer!

To every voice of recommendation... and their contribution to the accomplishment of this project... I am honored and grateful that you took the time. first to my Bishop... Bishop Dr. G. A. Thompson... thanks, Dad, for always believing in me and taking the time to write the foreword for this book.

To Dr Jerry Grillo... thank you for your recommendation. To Evangelist Debra George... thank you for your recommendation. To Pastor Matthew K. Thompson... thank you for your recommendation. To Phil Thompson... thank you for taking the time to write a recommendation while traveling the globe.

To my Victory Nation... Victory world church... thank you for giving me an audience to fulfill God's plan and purpose for my life and his kingdom.

Special thanks to my editor... Dr. E. Lee Caleca.

Thanks to my project manager... Ry An, Sienna Yazbek along with his entire team at the Book Writing Founders.

ABOUT THE AUTHOR

Keith Banks-Obanor (AKA PK) is also the author of the '162-Daily Devotional Book.' He's a motivational speaker and a life coach. He's the Lead Pastor of Victory World Church Int'l in Boston, MA, along with his wife, Sogie, and the visionary of Victory World Outreach Ministries, an outreach organization that extends its impact to nations like Uganda, Kenya, and Nigeria. He's the CEO of Aspire Holdings and Acquisitions / Aspire Publications. He obtained his ministerial training and education from LoveWorld Ministerial College (Christ Embassy) under the presbytery of Rev. Dr. Chris Oyakhilome, Lagos, Nigeria, and Gordon Conwell Theological Seminary, Boston, MA. His messages and writings are full of faith, hope, and inspiration that challenge anyone who comes in contact with him to go after their dreams. He carries an anointing that transcends boundaries and limitations to heal and change your world. PK is a prolific author and teacher of the Word. He operates dynamically in the prophetic, deliverance, and healing anointing. His authority in the Word of God always creates momentum for your breakthrough. He is a member of the City Harvest Network in good standing, under the pastoral covering and leadership of Dr. Rod Parsley at World Harvest Church in Columbus, Ohio. Keith was ordained as a minister of the gospel in 2001 under A Church Without Walls, Boston, MA, by Presiding Bishop G.A. Thompson. He is married to his choir sweetheart, Senior Pastor, and First Lady, Sogie Cynthia Banks-Obanor. They are blessed with three lovely children: Charisma, Sharon, and Joey.

INTRODUCTION

Fear causes emotional paralysis, worry is its twin, and anxiety is the seed of fear and worry. Let me show you in this book how to recognize the cause and navigate its negative effects on your overall well-being.

Are you an excessive or chronic worrier who always fears the worst in every situation?

Well, worry can affect your mind and body in unimaginable ways. According to WEB MD, excessive worrying can lead to feelings of high anxiety and panic attacks, which can cause physiological changes in your body that eventually lead to physical illness.[1] Psychologist Catherine Pittman and author Elizabeth Karle, in their book Rewire Your Anxious Brain, observed that the amygdala and cortex (both important parts of the brain) are the essential players in the neuropsychology of anxiety. The amygdala, they further explained, acts as a primal response, and frequently, when this part of the brain processes fear, you may not even understand why you are afraid. Unlike the amygdala, the cortex is the center of worry… that is, obsessing, ruminating, and dwelling on things that may or may not happen.[2]

This is known as catastrophic thinking or always predicting bad outcomes. And it's just as often not the threat itself but the perception

---

[1] Khatri, M. How worry affects your body. WebMD. https://www.webmd.com/anxiety-panic/ss/slideshow-worrybody-effects
[2] Pittman, C. M., & Karle, E. M. (2019). Rewire your anxious brain: How to use the neuroscience of fear to end anxiety, panic, & worry. Echo Point Books & Media.

of the stressor or threat, which suggests that modern stress is often self-induced. And that is the thrust of this book.

In one of his popular quotes, the late renowned TV evangelist and author Dr. Billy Graham said: "Historians will probably call our era the 'Age of anxiety.'"[3]

According to Dr. Graham, anxiety is the natural result when our hopes are centered on anything short of God and His will for us. Saint Mark's gospel chapter 4, verses 35-39, explains how Jesus peacefully slept in the boat… during the storm while the disciples panicked and worried themselves almost to death.

Mark 4:35-39:

> *"That day when evening came, he said to his disciples, "Let us go over to the other side." Leaving the crowd behind, they took him along, just as he was, in the boat. There were also other boats with him. A furious squall came up, and the waves broke over the boat, so that it was nearly swamped. Jesus was in the stern, sleeping on a cushion. The disciples woke him and said to him, "Teacher, don't you care if we drown?"*
>
> *He got up, rebuked the wind and said to the waves, "Quiet! Be still!" Then the wind died down and it was completely calm."*

The book of Acts chapter 12, verses 5-7, also records how Peter was kept in prison, bound by chains, sleeping between two soldiers, and suddenly God Almighty sent his angels to break the chains off because of the church's prayers. I am sure Peter went to bed with an assurance of hope and trust in the one who could rescue him from his dilemma.

---

3 Graham, B. (1965). World aflame. Garden City, NY: Doubleday.

Acts 12:5-7:

> *"So Peter was kept in prison, but the church was earnestly praying to God for him. The night before Herod was to bring him to trial, Peter was sleeping between two soldiers, bound with two chains, and sentries stood guard at the entrance. Suddenly, an angel of the Lord appeared and a light shone in the cell. He struck Peter on the side and woke him up. "Quick, get up!" he said, and the chains fell off Peter's wrists."*

Most recent research shows how certain negativeemotional states of mind due to excessive worrying and anxiety could harm our health and overall well-being. It might be obvious that Peter was not worried or anxious over his predicament. He had faith and was, therefore, able to sleep soundly.

Here are just some of the ways stress, worry, and negative emotions can affect you physiologically:

Anger weakens your liver

Stress weakens your heart and brain

Worry weakens your stomach

Grief weakens your lungs

Fear weakens your kidney

Hacking Your Happiness Chemicals

Your state of mind—being happy or unhappy—can affect everything you do. When you're happy, you're naturally more productive and more motivated. It's easier to bear daily difficulties and challenges.

And your energy can affect other people.

But if you think you're doing everything right to make yourself happy but just can't seem to get it right, maybe it's not what you're doing or not doing that's causing the problem.

It might be your happiness chemicals—the 4 neurotransmitters responsible for that elevated feeling of well-being.

Neurotransmitters can be naturally triggered, but sometimes, we need to give them a little help.

Hacking into your happiness chemicals is easy, but don't get too much of a good thing. Just like any addictive substance, these naturally occurring neurochemicals, although completely safe, can have the same addictive effect.

According to the *Mind Journal*, here are more observations on "happiness" chemicals and how to hack them.[4]

DOPAMINE—The Reward Chemical

The brain contains what's known as the reward pathway, and the brain chemical most closely associated with the brain's reward stimuli is dopamine. If you're depressed or lack the motivation to do anything, there's a good chance you're deficient in dopamine.

You get a shot of dopamine when you do things that make you feel good. Each time you do that same thing, whether eating pie or watching a great movie, you reinforce that pleasure.

---

4   Rose, A. (2023, January 31). Happiness Chemicals and how to Hack Them. The Minds Journal. https://themindsjournal.com/quotes/happiness-chemicalsand-how-to-hack-them/

Your brain will tell you to take that action again to get more reward, the reward being dopamine, the 'feel good' hormone.

The dopamine is the final effect, but the memory of that feeling will cause you to repeat the action that made you feel good.

And you don't need to do this with only one item, action, or project. Create small celebrations that reinforce what you've done and your accomplishments. Keep small goals going so you'll have a consistent source of potential dopamine, such as:

Completing a task

Doing self-care activities

Eating comfort food

Celebrating little wins

You can help others get a shot of dopamine by recognizing their accomplishments or throwing them an honest compliment, which is a great way to motivate people to do their best.

OXYTOCIN—The Love Hormone

The love or cuddle hormone is the main function of oxytocin during and after childbirth. It's considered critical for social bonding. If you want to raise your oxytocin level, reach out and touch someone. Hug them, get a shoulder massage from a friend, or cuddle a baby.

You can get more oxytocin by:

Playing with a dog

Playing with a baby

Holding the hand of a loved one, child, or friend

Hugging your family

Giving compliments

And you'll be doing your heart good, literally. Higher oxytocin levels reduce stress and strengthen the immune system.

SEROTONIN—The Mood Stabilizer

Depression and loneliness are possible signs of low serotonin levels. Also known as 5-hydroxytryptamine (5-HT), psychotherapists have long given drugs that simulate the effects of serotonin: Prozac, Paxil, and Zoloft, for example. Ecstasy is another source of artificial serotonin.

These drugs have been prescribed to stabilize mood, but these artificial sources prohibit the flood of this hormone from being reabsorbed into the body, which can leave the brain damaged.

To naturally increase your serotonin level, get the full spectrum of B vitamins and eat eggs, cheese, nuts, and turkey. These foods contain tryptophan, the precursor to serotonin.

Expose yourself to a little sunshine. UV rays promote Vitamin D and serotonin by absorbing through the skin. Limit your time to about 20 minutes of full sunlight or until your skin turns a little pink.

Other ways to induce serotonin production include:

Meditating

Running

Walk in nature

Swimming

Cycling

ENDORPHINS—The Pain Killer

Endorphins are a group of hormones that trigger the body's opiate receptors and also act as sedatives. They have a pain-killing effect. But in addition to this, they can prompt a positive feeling, something runners call a runner's high.

What are the best ways to release endorphins? Exercise and laughter.

Find things to laugh at, share your sense of humor, and get regular exercise. It doesn't matter what kind, as long as it's sustainable for 20-30 minutes daily. If you're looking for happiness, give some thought to your actions. Ask yourself if an experience is going to be beneficial for all parties concerned. Will it create a feeling of unity, acceptance, and happiness?

Our energy, human energy, can be very powerful. As you go through life—experiencing life—remember that this is not all there is.

Mastering the art of love for all things. In this way, you will find the energy of happiness.

    Laughter

    Exercise

    Essential oils

    Watch a comedy

    Dark chocolate

Let's get into the why of a life of worry, stress, fear and anxiety.

CHAPTER ONE

YOU ARE NOT WIRED FOR A LIFE OF WORRY

Everything made—everything designed or created is wired to function according to what it was designed or built for.

Your car is wired and designed for transportation.

Your house is designed and built for habitation.

Your kitchen stove is designed and wired to cook your food.

But humans are *not* wired to live a life of worry and fear.

Psalms 139:14 says, *"We have been fearfully and wonderfully made in God's own image."*

God designed and wired us with an original intent of being instruments of worship, praise and exaltation to the glory of his name.

PK'S PILL… the existence of any product is to fulfill the purpose of its original intent.

God is our manufacturer, and we are his products, so as you read this book, let me re-program, rewire… and equip you to overcome the dysfunction of worry in your life today.

Facts You Should Know About Worry

Definition: WORRY

1. To give yourself away from anxiety or to be in a state where you are not at ease.

2. To allow one's mind to dwell on difficulty or troubles.

3. To agonize oneself by getting all worked up or tormenting oneself and losing sleep.

4. A mental state of distress or agitation resulting from concern, usually for something impending or anticipated.

As you can see, WORRY can be defined in several ways, but none are good or healthy for our state of being. Instead of being optimistic and anticipating the best of all situations and God's 'favor,' you unequivocally anticipate the worst by being a pessimist.

The Greek word for Worry is *merimnao*, the same root word for anxiety. That is why some translations of Philippians *4: 6-7* say*:*

"Be anxious for nothing."

The New Living Bible translates it this way:

"Don't worry about anything; instead, pray about everything. Tell God what you need and thank him for all he has done."

I will take the liberty to expand more on Philippians 4 briefly.

**Worry is also a wrong persuasion that
ultimately destroys the winner's world.**

Your world is your garden—worry will stop the growth of any good seed planted in your garden's soil or mind. Your mind is your world. Most times, the negative—intrusive thoughts entertained in our minds—can be the most troubling, disturbing, and detrimental to our peace of mind.

Worry is a wrong focus that produces negative energy.

**Worry is an opinion that your enemy
is more powerful than you.**

**Worry is confidence in your adversary —
but worship is confidence in God.**

Worry is definitely a burden that you cannot heal.

Worry replaced by prayer is a total trust in God.

You can only do what you can know what you know— control whatever circumstances are within your power and ability.

Our Lord and Savior Jesus Christ himself admonishes His disciples in Matthew 6:27 (New International version):

*"…which one of you by worrying can
add a single hour to your life?"*

We live in a culture where stress is the order of the day. Either we are alarmed about global politics or rumors of wars and the catastrophes of earthquakes and hurricanes, or we're stressed over unpaid bills, meeting our sales quotas at work, or a cranky boss in the office.

We are worried and weary about losing our jobs—we are over-extended, running on empty—and it doesn't take long before fear sets in and anxiety takes its toll on us. Anxiety disorder comprises the most mental illness in America—18% of the adult population is widely affected.

Worry, fear, and anxiety are inseparable spirits and negative emotions that operate together.

Whenever a person begins to worry and fear the unknown, chances are the *spirit or the emotion of anxiety is in operation.*

The tangible manifestation of worry and anxiety usually initiates fear in a person.

I am convinced that living your life in uncertainty and being double-minded is the breeding ground for a lifestyle of worrying and living in fear.

You see, the things that make us worry and fearful frequently *appear* to be real, when in reality, it is usually false evidence that is making it appear real and convincing—like a mirage, an optical illusion caused by atmospheric conditions, for instance, or the appearance of a sheet of water on a hot road caused by the refraction of light from the sky by heated air.

Stress has always been around. It's a normal psychological and physiological reaction to the demands of life. People experience severe stress-inducing challenges every year, and many have some type of stress every day. But it may shock many that worrying and being concerned are two different concepts.

Don't Worry About It: Go to Bed

You can derive positive energy from being concerned.

Being concerned usually drives you to search for options and solutions.

I'll give you an example. If I was concerned that my son Joey might not have enough funds left in his college account portfolio to pay for his college tuition, being concerned regarding the situation becomes my motivating factor to do something about it, like finding ways to create extra cash flow. On the contrary, sitting down and doing nothing about my son's college situation and worrying and becoming fearful and hopeless that he might get kicked out of school only creates a negative energy, leading to anxiety and depression or a feeling of failure and inadequacy.

My friend, author Dr. Jerry Grillo, observes, "Worry is a concern out of control."

World-renowned American actor Will Smith observes that "Fear is not real."

The only place that fear can exist is in our thoughts of the Future—it is a product of our imagination, causing us to fear Things that are not at present and may never exist. The danger is very real—but fear is a choice. You were not designed or wired to live in fear and worry because God our maker knows more about our make-up and how he wired us as humans…he gave us these instructions in his word in Philippians 4:6-7:

> *"Do not be anxious about anything, but in every situation, by prayer and petition, with thanksgiving, present your requests to God. And the peace of God, which transcends all understanding, will guard your hearts and your minds in Christ Jesus."*

In verse 8 of the same chapter, we are told what to focus on:

"Finally, brothers: whatever things are true, whatever things are honest, whatever is just, whatever things are pure, whatever things are lovely, whatever things are of good report, if there is any virtue and if any praise, think about these things."

Apparently, from the list of things the Bible admonishes us to focus and think on, it shows that if we can get our minds to meditate and ponder on the positive things, our journey to living a worry and fear-free life is inevitable.

Author and motivational speaker Les Brown observes:

"Too many of us are not living our dreams because we are living our fears."

World-renowned leadership coach and New York Times best-selling author John C. Maxwell quotes:

"The greatest mistake we make is living constantly, fearing we will make one."

Helpful Tips For Mental Illness

Mental illness is real. Awareness of this terrible disorder could be the beginning of finding a cure.

Nutrition, exercise, spiritual and mental counseling, and surrounding yourself with positive people and a great support system play a big role in creating healthy mental well-being. But one key villain also plays a role in this debilitating disorder: mood swings.

And you must learn to:

Take control of your mood-swings

Your mood swings are like having another individual living in you… a stranger that takes over, something you have a difficult time controlling. But if you do not take control of these manifested behavioral patterns, they will dominate and disrupt your mental well-being, affecting your entire life.

So how do you do that?

Mood swings are the result of hormonal imbalances. As much as you may have heard this before for several disorders, a proper healthy diet and exercise can go a long way to helping you balance your hormones.

Diet & Exercise

There's a lot to know about eating healthy, but it comes down to eating whole foods, as God intended. Of course, it would be almost impossible today for anyone to grow all their food and raise their animals, but there's a lot you *can* do.

Covering everything there is to know about healthy eating and today's food would require an entire book, but here are some basic dietary guidelines that I believe are correct. You'll find they contrast the politically correct dietary guidelines set out by "experts."

Please remember that I am not giving you medical advice but merely suggestions on eating healthy foods to help balance your moods and emotions.

I Timothy 4:4-5 tells us, *"For everything God created is good, and nothing is to be rejected if it is received with thanksgiving, because it is consecrated by the word of God and prayer."*

The danger of the politically correct guidelines when understanding food is that they are based on **prepackaged**, **preserved**, **adulterated**, and **modified foods**. These are not foods as God created them.

Let's look at what these same foods in their natural state can provide.

Saturated Fats - Fats provide cell membrane integrity and enhance the body's ability to use essential fatty acids. They protect the liver and are the preferred food for the heart. They do not cause heart disease.

Dietary Cholesterol - Contrary to what we're told, we need cholesterol. It contributes to the strength of the intestinal wall and helps babies and children develop healthy brain and nervous systems. Foods that contain cholesterol also contain other nutrients. Only oxidized cholesterol contributes to heart disease. Powdered milk and powdered eggs contain oxidized cholesterol; powdered milk is added to 1% and 2% milk.

Polyunsaturates are new to the human diet due to modernization and mechanization. They contribute to learning disabilities, intestinal problems, heart disease, cancer, and autoimmune diseases, among other things.

Grass Fed Red Meat (not grain-fed) - There's a difference. Modern grains lack the digestible proteins of ancient grains. Grass-fed animals provide meat that is a rich source of nutrients, including vitamins B12, B6, zinc, phosphorus, carnitine, and coenzyme Q10, which protect the heart and nervous system.

Eggs - Remember the incredible edible egg campaign? Eggs provide excellent protein and many important fatty acids that contribute to the health of the brain and nervous system. Americans had less heart disease when they ate more eggs. Egg substitutes have been shown to cause rapid death in test animals.

Lowfat and Nonfat Milk - These products lack fatsoluble vitamins needed to assimilate the protein and minerals in the milk itself. Consumption of low-fat foods (foods with the fat removed, not foods that are naturally low in fat) can lead to depletion of vitamins A and D.

30% of Calories as fat is too low for most people and can lead to low blood sugar and fatigue. Before the mechanization of foods, traditional diets contained 40% to 80% of calories from fat, mostly from animal origins. The difference was that the animals were not pumped with steroids, hormones, antibiotics, and pesticide-laden processed feed. Toxins are stored in the fatty tissue of animals (including humans), so a clean animal will contain clean fat.

Most **Grain Products** are made from wheat flour, which has been processed and refined, bleached and stripped, leaving it devoid of nutrients. Modern wheat is a hybrid, containing newer proteins thought to trigger inflammatory responses, nutrient deficiencies and intestinal problems, including Celiac disease. Try using **spelt flour**, an **ancient grain** in the wheat family.

Salt or **sodium** is crucial to digestion and assimilation. Many foods contain naturally occurring sodium and should not be avoided. Rock or mineral salt contains a higher percentage of sodium than potassium.

Sea salt contains a higher percentage of potassium than sodium. The cells need potassium and sodium on the outside to maintain a proper balance and function.

Fruits and Vegetables (plants) receive an average of 10 applications of pesticides during their growing and storage lifetime.

Modern Soy Products (another hybrid) block mineral absorption, inhibit protein digestion, depress thyroid function, and contain potent carcinogens.

WebMD suggests the following:[5]

Include fiber, nutrients, lean protein, good fats, and whole complex carbohydrates. They explain that regularly eating breakfast can improve mood, memory, and energy and promote feelings of calmness.

Exercise

Moving your body in any way keeps everything internally flowing. Stretching, walking, bending, lifting, doing household chores, and gardening are good forms of exercise.

"Exercise to stimulate, not to annihilate." – Lee Haney

Set small goals for yourself, such as working in the garden for 30 minutes or walking for ten minutes twice daily. Make your exercise challenging but not overwhelming.

---

5   Newman, D. (2018). The benefits of eating breakfast. WebMD. https://www.webmd.com/diet/features/many-benefitsbreakfast#:~:text=Control%20Blood%20Sugar,which%20can%20lead%20to%20diabetes.

Getting Professional Help

We can only do so much to keep ourselves healthy through food and exercise. If you still have difficulty controlling your mood swings, finding a qualified medical professional to guide you further is a good idea.

CHAPTER TWO

12 WAYS THAT LIFE GETS YOU TO WORRY

'Life is not fair.'

Some of the greatest lessons learned in life are learned in the heat of our struggles and battles. *"Your victory and growth are measured by the battles you endure and overcome."*

Life is not fair, they say. This statement was coined because life never seems to treat us fairly—regardless of our background, ethnicity, disposition or expectations. The good book says in Matthew 5:45:

> "…that you may be children of your Father in heaven.
> He causes his sun to rise on the evil and the good and
> sends rain on the righteous and the unrighteous."

> "Life is not fair because… life would not give you
> what you deserve, but rather what you demand."

So demand something out of life… go for it, fight for it!

America's renowned author and motivational speaker Les Brown quotes:

> "Life is a fight for territory… and once you stop fighting for what you want… what you don't want will automatically take over."

Someone rightly said that the greatest teacher of all time is life itself. Life, they say, teaches us a lesson that cannot be learned in the classroom… but on the battlefield. Life has a way of molding and shaping us into better individuals… it also gets us to worry about the unknown. When we live an unproductive life full of endless routines, boredom is bound to set in.

A life that can be predictable by the hour or day has ceased to be adventurous. They say that the true definition of insanity is doing the same thing repeatedly and expecting a different result. So why are you doing the same thing repeatedly and expecting a different result? If nothing is changing for you, perhaps you are your problem.

TV Evangelist and author Dr. Mike Murdock quotes:

> "You will never change your life until you change something you do daily."

The 12 Ways That Life Gets You to Worry and Be Anxious

1. A distorted picture and fear of the unknown

Life has a way of painting you a distorted picture, creating a negative feeling of that which you fear the most. Life gets us to worry about the unknown, the uncertainty and the vicissitudes—the unwelcome changes in our circumstances—that we encounter along life's journey.

2. Inadequate information or knowledge about the next level or season of your life

Not having enough information and the right knowledge to aspire to the next level of your life could cripple your zeal and enthusiasm for life. Hosea 4:6: *"My people are destroyed from lack of knowledge. Because you have rejected knowledge, I also reject you as my priests; because you have ignored the law of your God, I also will ignore your children."*

3. Feeling I Insecure

We become insecure when we anticipate being displaced from our position or status. This feeling can be overwhelming! When we feel someone may know or do better than us, we tend to put on our guide, becoming vulnerable and losing the joy and pride of being original rather than a cheap copy… someone we are not.

4. Lack of trust for others…especially when you have been hurt

The saying 'once bitten-twice shy' is so true when dealing with the issue of trust. It takes a lot to trust again once you have been hurt, especially by those closest to you. Sometimes, people can also develop trust issues when they become paranoid or insecure in different areas. Romantic relationships are a good example because just about everyone has had one. If you were rejected, you might be shy of getting into another relationship because your *fear* of rejection limits your view. But this can also apply to taking calculated risks. If you've invested money in a project that went sour, you might be unwilling to invest in another one, even after your research. You've lost *trust* in your ability to make sound decisions.

Living on the edge because of your insecurities— trying to prove something to yourself—is the unhealthiest way to live. You're living without boundaries, which could harm you in many ways.

However, setting boundaries for yourself should not mean you're limiting yourself. Look at why you've lost trust in life, people, yourself, and your abilities. Then, use the rational part of your brain to determine if your actions are a calculated risk or a completely wild one without sound prospects. You only have one life to live, so live it to the fullest and learn to trust again.

5. Refusing to let go and let God take over

God becomes unnecessary whenever we choose to be the master and architect of our lives. We are reminded in these Bible texts of our dependence upon God as humans:

Romans 8:28:

> *"And we know that in all things God works for the good of those who love him, who have been called according to his purpose."*

Proverbs 16:9:

> *"In their hearts, humans plan their course, but the Lord establishes their steps."*

6. Trying to live up to people's expectations

Being a people pleaser is possibly the worst thing you could do in trying to live a worry and anxiety-free life. In my line of business and ministry, I have often heard the resounding voice of many of my mentors saying, "Son, you can't make everyone happy." Trying to please people is an endless task that depletes your energy… so don't even try. Whatever you do to try to please people will never be enough. That doesn't mean you shouldn't be kind and helpful, but do it for the right reasons. The right reason is to simply be helpful when someone is in need. The wrong reason is to appease your sense of self-worth, wanting people to "like" you.

So, using all of the above strategies, the enemy can distract you by getting you to focus on your prevailing circumstances, filling your head with fear, doubts, worry and questions about what your tomorrow holds. For example, inadequate information and knowledge about the next season of your life could worry you to death because you can't know WHEN, WHERE and HOW it will all unfold. Truth be told, you wouldn't be able to leave where you are now until you know where you are going. You'd be stunted, limited, and stuck.

7. Letting your emotions rule your faith

This is another strategy; emotions and faith are the two most powerful forces that rule us as humans.

In the land of **emotions**, we **worry**. We **fear** the worst, and we **panic**.

But in the land of **faith**, we **believe**, **hope**, and are **steadfast**.

I am reminded of the serenity prayer written by Reinhold Niebuhr in 1971:

> "God grant me the serenity to accept the things I
> cannot change, the courage to change the things I
> can, and the wisdom to know the difference."

8. Imagining the worst

Imagining the bad, the ugly, and the worst things happening to you, having a negative mental attitude instead of a positive mental attitude, or even being afraid of the future and the unknown are probably the most effective tools the enemy uses to get us to worry the most. Your mind is like a computer programmed by the environment you grew up in. The pain and sorrow that we are inflicted within our lives, either as a direct result of the separation or divorce of a parent, the loss of a loved one, or the disappointments we encounter in our career and relationships, could, over the years become like compound interest, that creates in us a negative mindset of fearing the worst and worrying about the unknown.

9. Self-pity or feeling sorry for yourself

This negative emotion creates a sense of abandonment and hopelessness in you. You unequivocally conclude that no one will ever understand the troubles and pain that you've been through. Self-pity or feeling sorry for yourself is mainly used to seek the attention of others, whether the attention-seeker is aware of it or not. When they fall short of making you feel better about yourself, you hold them in resentment because of your insecurities, and it reinforces the idea that no one understands you and your troubles.

10. Letting your past dictate your future

The weight of your past is too heavy to bring into your present or future!!

Whenever you allow your past issues to corrode your present mindset and its creativity, you indirectly create a recipe for disaster that'll hinder your ability to see a brighter and promising future. There's a reason why your windshield is bigger than your rearview mirror. The reason is that the future—what's ahead of you—is so much bigger and brighter than the past behind you. Where you are going is so much better than where you've been.

It is harder to move forward if you keep looking back at your past. Have you ever tried walking with your head turned to what's behind you? It's much harder to do than if your head and eyes are forward on what's in front of you. So hold your head up, and keep looking ahead.

And for the record, just because things went wrong before doesn't mean they will go wrong again, either in your business ventures or trying to find happiness in your relationships. Every failure can afford you the opportunity to learn a life lesson and gain some insight and wisdom. You are supposed to learn from your mistakes and prepare yourself to take the next giant leap of faith. *So goes the saying—*

"What doesn't kill you makes you stronger and wiser."

In my previous book, *Your 162 Daily Devotional,* I quote:

> "God will never consult your past to create
> a brighter and better future for you."

The prophet Isaiah also alluded to this concept about your past. Isaiah 43:18-20:

> *"Forget the former things; do not dwell on the past.*
> *See, I am doing a new thing! Now it springs up;*
> *do you not perceive it? I am making a way in the*
> *wilderness and streams in the wasteland.*
>
> *"The wild animals honor me, the jackals and the owls,*
> *because I provide water in the wilderness and streams in*
> *the wasteland to give drink to my people, my chosen."*

Letting your past dictate your future could also negatively impact you by making you live in total disbelief and doubt that you still have some of the best days ahead. This can create a perpetual state of worry, anxiety, and inability to grasp that the person you were in the past has nothing to do with who you are now, today, and who you will be tomorrow… the new you.

11. Guilty Conscience

Guilt is a terrible burden to bear!! It cuts like a knife and eats your soul like cancer! The things you go through in life can, over time, put a heavy burden of unworthiness, shame and guilt on you.

The following text in Saint Matthew's gospel and the Old Testament book of Isaiah are both rich nuggets for the soul when dealing with a heavy burden, guilt and shame:

Matthew 11:28-30:

"Come to me, all you who are weary and burdened, and I will give you rest. Take my yoke upon you and learn from me, for I am gentle and humble in heart, and you will find rest for your souls. For my yoke is easy and my burden is light."

Isaiah 1:18:

"Come now, let us settle the matter," says the Lord. "Though your sins are like scarlet, they shall be as white as snow; though they are red as crimson, they shall be like wool."

12. Lack and inadequacy mentality

A mentality of lack and inadequacy—meaning a mindset of not having enough—is a disease that can infect and disenfranchise your ability to prosper and do well. Poverty is a thing of the mind!! We become what we think about most. You become that which you focus your attention on.

"You'll never grow beyond your self-limiting thoughts."

As a matter of fact, the Bible says in Proverbs 23:7:

> *"For he is the kind of person who is always thinking about the cost. 'Eat and drink,' he says to you, but his heart is not with you."*

Said differently in the King James Version, Proverbs 23:7:

> *For as he thinketh in his heart, so is he: Eat and drink, saith he to thee; but his heart is not with thee."*

Napoleon Hill, in his bestseller book Think and Grow Rich, quotes:

> "The starting point of all achievement is DESIRE."

Keep this constantly in mind. Weak desire brings weak results, just as a small fire makes a small amount of heat.

> "Whatever the mind can conceive and believe, it can achieve."
> —Napoleon Hill

CHAPTER THREE

FAITH OVER FEAR

...when faith walks out, fear sets in

The Pandemic

While in the process of writing this book, depending on when you pick it up to read, our world got hit with a deadly airborne virus... code name COVID-19, also known as 'CORONA VIRUS DISEASE 2019'. This global pandemic rocked our world with so much fear and uncertainty. It affected almost every country in the world. When I was on this chapter on March 31st, 2020, there had been a total of 786,332 cases and an astronomical number of 37,830 deaths reported worldwide up to that point. By the time I was done publishing this book, the death toll had risen to the millions.[6]

Where and How It All Began

According to the South Morning China Post, a 55 years old individual from Hubei province in China may have been the first person to have

---

6 World Health Organization. Who coronavirus (COVID-19) dashboard. World Health Organization. https://covid19.who.int/

contacted COVID-19, which was more than a month earlier than doctors first noted cases in Wuhan, China, which is in Hubei province.[7]

By March 2020, this deadly disease had spread across the globe. In the U.S., local and non-essential businesses and schools were shut down. Movie theaters and houses of worship were forced to close their doors to prohibit a wider spread of the airborne virus. Social distancing became the new norm… family quarantines became the order of the day. People were afraid to leave their homes… and afraid of their future. The nation's symbol of wealth, Wall Street, was down to the lowest it's ever been since the Great Depression of 1929. Unemployment was at its highest rate. Numerous small businesses went out of business for lack of trade.

Hopelessness and uncertainty overwhelmingly swept across America and other countries.

Fear gripped people around the world.

Fear of losing their homes and jobs.

Fear of not getting proper treatment if diagnosed with the virus because of the lack of medical tools like masks, ventilators and beds.

Fear of losing a loved one to the deadly virus.

Fear of being robbed of their possessions by desperate others.

Fear of the world as we know it is ending.

---

[7] Ma, J. (2021, May 10). Exclusive: China's first confirmed covid-19 case traced back to November 17. South China Morning Post. https://www.scmp.com/news/china/society/article/3074991/coronavirus-chinas-first-confirmed-covid-19-case-traced-back

Even when a vaccine became available in late 2020 / early 2021, the world faced another fear: fear of the vaccination itself. What was supposed to be a remedy for protection against the deadly virus became a political issue that created a great divide. Many held a different view and opinion about the safety of the Pfizer, Moderna and Johnson and Johnson drugs, the main leading brands of the Covid-19 vaccines.

Many who opted out of getting vaccinated were forced out of their jobs and schools.

The World LIVED IN FEAR!

When fear sets in—faith walks out—

> *"All men have fears, but the brave ones put down their fears and go forward, sometimes to death but always to victory…"*

This was the model of the king's guard in Ancient Greece.

The 7 Most Basic Fears Known to Mankind

Fear is a negative emotion. Though a wide range of fear plagues us as humans, I believe these are the seven most basic fears that plague humans.

1. **The fear of poverty**: The fear of poverty can overtake one's mind by painting a picture of never having enough or losing the little you have someday. How will I feed my children? Will I lose my home? How will I pay my bills? Will we be out on the street? It's accompanied by shame and a sense of failure, of not being good enough. This fear can be overwhelmingly daunting. But it could create in you a negative or positive kind of energy that will drive you to make decisions—either motivating you to do more, to

make decisions that will keep you moving forward or bring you up, or to continue in a downward spiral that will reinforce your fear of lack or poverty. This fear might create a negative energy in you, driving you to amass ill-gotten wealth or treasure or a positive energy that will eventually lead to developing a million-dollar idea.

2. **The fear of ill health**: This fear can actually *lead* to sickness. Someone so afraid of becoming ill that they constantly dwell on that can actually make themselves sick. Remember, what you set your mind on, what you focus on most, is what will show up in your life.

3. **The fear of criticism**: This fear can rob us of our confidence and lead us to live an antisocial lifestyle. Don't isolate yourself. If you have people in your life who are critical in a harmful way, remove those people from your life.

4. **The fear of the loss of love**: This fear is what drives people from one relationship to the other. They become unstable in their love life and can't seem to love freely. They are stuck in old patterns, bringing the past into every relationship, expecting to lose. And what happens? Their behavior manifests into the relationship they expect: rejection and loss.

5. **The fear of the loss of liberty**: This fear can create a sense of bondage. People who fear losing their liberty become attached to the lifestyle keeping them bound. Their fear of losing what they believe is their freedom or liberty keeps them from stretching, seeking, and being adventurous in life.

6. **The fear of old age**: The reality of growing old someday does not resonate well with the human psyche. And in the words of the soft rock legend Rod Stewart, we all want to live 'forever young.'

7. **The fear of death:** Benjamin Franklin once said in a letter written to Jean Baptiste Leroy, a prominent scientist in 1789, that 'The only two certainties in life are Death and Taxes. We've all heard this, and regardless of whether or not you can avoid paying taxes, no one can avoid physical death on this earth. So why fear it?

Sadly, the fear of old age and death has haunted humans since the fall of man in the Garden of Eden when Adam and Eve committed treason.

But…

Fear Changes Nothing!

A life lived in fear is one lived in bondage to those fears.

If doubt and unbelief are the opposite of faith, then fear must be the opposite of confidence, trust and assurance. The Bible says in Proverbs 3:5 (New International Version):

> *"Trust in the Lord with all your heart and lean not on your own understanding…in all thy ways submit to him (or acknowledge him), and he will make your paths straight."*

Another translation says, *"…he'll direct thy paths."*

Proverbs 28:1 (New International Version) says:

> *"The wicked flee though no one pursues, but the righteous are as bold as a lion."*

The state of being confident is definitely a proven concept that our fear could not in any way contend with. The apostle Paul alluded to this when he wrote to the Philippian church.

Philippians 1:6 (American Standard Version):

"…being confident of this very thing, that he who began a good work in you will perfect it until the day of Jesus Christ."

The English dictionary defines 'confidence' as a feeling of trust and firm belief in yourself or others. May I suggest that true and total confidence in a higher power that supersedes human power and human ability is the true definition of faith? So whenever we put our confidence in a fickle mortal man who's unstable in his ways, fear sets in, and faith walks out. Why? Because man's ways and attributes are synonymous with fear and uncertainty, God's ways are synonymous with faith, hope and surety.

The Bible talks about faith in Hebrews 11:1:

"…the substance of things hoped for… the evidence of things not seen."

Hoping for what you do not yet possess physical evidence for is actually putting your faith into action.

Whenever you decide to operate by faith, you will always stand the chance of contending with the force of fear.

Faith and fear cannot coexist because fear will demoralize you and paralyze your ability to see beyond where you are and where you'd rather be—to where you strive to be. Fear can even stop you from beginning the journey. You will never reach your destination, or you can't even begin. You're stuck. Fear will limit you to the familiar, the safety net, and your comfort zone. It will hold you back from exploring what your curiosity tells you to explore and from venturing out into the unknown and unfamiliar. But faith, on the other hand, would propel you to go beyond every limitation and discover your potential.

If you drive from New Jersey to California at night, you will have your headlights on, but you can only see 100 yards in front of you. You drive by faith, knowing the road will continue every 100 yards. You don't stop the car and check to see if the road is still there.

Faith creates in you the boldness, inspiration, determination, and drive to discover what could be, explore the possibilities, and realize that a victory exists on the other side of your battle. And like all battles, we must go through them; we can't go around them.

Faith and Fear Cannot Coexist

Furthermore, faith and fear cannot coexist because God can only deal with us as humans through the concept of faith. Hebrews 11:6 (New International Version) gives us clarity on this.

> *"And without faith, it is impossible to please God, because anyone who comes to him must first believe that he exists and that he rewards those who earnestly or diligently seek him."*

In Luke, chapter 8, verses 22–25, the Bible records how a fierce storm came against the ship Jesus and the disciples took to cross to the other side of the lake. Though Jesus was on the ship with them and their faith was based on the things that the master had taught them, they needed to be tried in its practicality. That's why, when they woke him because they were terrified, Jesus asked them the question (verse 25):

> *"Where is your faith?"*

Pk's wisdom pill:

> "Anytime God gets ready to take you to the other side in life, there will always be a storm that comes

> to test and challenge your faith, your trust and
> total dependence upon Him and His word."

Permit me to interject this for a moment… you see, the best time to build your faith is not during a storm but before the storm. Because when the storm comes, it will eventually reveal the real you… your frailty, your weaknesses, or your strengths. Our storms and trials always reveal what we are made of… our substance and values.

Whenever we are faced with challenges and adversity as humans, we are usually faced with these three choices:

1. You can decide to give in to fear, worry and anxiety.

2. You can decide to trust a man, the government or your education.

3. You can decide to pray about it, leave it in God's hands, and let the devil know that you no longer have the time to worry about it.

And then go to bed. Why?

Because your Bible says in Psalm 121:8:

> *"The Lord will watch over your coming and
> going both now and forevermore."*

Proverbs 15:3:

> *"The eyes of the Lord are everywhere, keeping
> watch on the wicked and the good."*

Don't Worry About It: Go to Bed

Psalm 91:1-2 (Authorized King James Version) (AKJV):

"He that dwelleth in the secret place of the most High shall abide under the shadow of the Almighty. I will say of the Lord, He is my refuge and my fortress: my God; in him will I trust."

There's a Fourth Man in the Fire!!

The story told of the three Hebrew boys, Shadrach, Meshach and Abednego, in Daniel 3:8-18, is an interesting one in that it depicts a total reliance and trust in Jehovah Nissi - God our Deliverer. The confidence and faith these three Hebrew boys demonstrated in the God they served was definitively uncompromising. There was not an iota of fear or worry in these boys. Let's take a minute to read and examine the text.

Daniel 3:16-18:

"Shadrach, Meshach and Abednego replied to him, "King Nebuchadnezzar, we do not need to defend ourselves before you in this matter. If we are thrown into the blazing furnace, the God we serve is able to deliver us from it, and he will deliver us[a] from Your Majesty's hand. But even if he does not, we want you to know, Your Majesty, that we will not serve your gods or worship the image of gold you have set up."

In verse 18 of this text, it seems that these boys were operating from the standpoint of faith over worry and fear that they were willing to risk their lives for what they believed. They would rather die believing in a blessed assurance than live another day having to serve an unknown, powerless god who cannot save them.

Verse 24–28 tells us how the story played out. The God of Shadrach, Meshach, and Abednego definitely came through for them. The presence of God represented the fourth man in the fire, whom the fire-stokers claimed they saw. Deliverance came to these three Hebrew boys because they trusted in a God that never fails. The Bible records that not even the hair on their body was burnt. They experienced the manifestation and reality of Psalms 23:4–6 in their lives!

Psalm 23:4-6 (King James Version):

"Yea, though I walk through the valley of the shadow of death, I will fear no evil: for thou art with me; thy rod and thy staff they comfort me.

Thou preparest a table before me in the presence of mine enemies: thou anointest my head with oil; my cup runneth over.

Surely goodness and mercy shall follow me all the days of my life: and I will dwell in the house of the Lord forever."

The 4th verse of this 23rd Psalm talks about walking through the valley of the shadow of death. The American English dictionary says a valley is a noun. It is a low land area between hills or mountains, typically with a river or stream flowing through it. This implies that though you could be in a valley today… at the very bottom, at your lowest point in life… keep your head high. Don't wear yourself out by worrying excessively because you could stop the flow of the river or stream that is flowing through you and in you. You could stop the flow of the rivers of living waters and the joy of experiencing the abundant life of almighty God. Jesus said it this way in John 7:38:

"Whoever believes in me, as Scripture has said, rivers of living water will flow from within them."

Faith and Fear Thrive on Information

Both faith and fear thrive on information received and believed. The knowledge received brings about an understanding, but the information received brings about a transformation. The Bible clearly says in Hosea 4:6:

> *"...my people are destroyed from lack of knowledge. Because you have rejected knowledge, I also reject you as my priests; because you have ignored the law of your God, I also will ignore your children."*

Also, the apostle Paul, in his letter to the Roman church, referenced how what we hear through information could impact our faith.

Romans 10:17:

> *"Consequently, faith comes from hearing the message, and the message is heard through the word about Christ."*

In the book of Numbers 13, the Bible gives an account of the spies that Moses sent out to spy on the land of Canaan, and the spies, except for Joshua and Caleb, brought back negative reports. This negative information that was passed on to the people was what brought fear to the people.

Numbers 13:27-29:

> *"They gave Moses this account: "We went into the land to which you sent us, and it does flow with milk and honey! Here is its fruit. But the people who live there are powerful, and the cities are fortified and very large. We even saw descendants of Anak there. The Amalekites live in the Negev; the Hittites, Jebusites and Amorites live in the hill country; and the Canaanites live near the sea and along the Jordan."*

Verse 32 of the same chapter says:

"And they spread among the Israelites a bad report about the land they had explored. They said, "The land we explored devours those living in it. All the people we saw there are of great size."

What we hear has the magnetic power to paint us a picture in our subconscious mind. Bad news has a way of conforming your mind to negative thoughts, while good news has a way of conforming to positive thoughts.

CHAPTER FOUR

IT IS ALL IN YOUR HEAD

There's a monster in the dark!

I remember growing up in my uncle's house; back home in the motherland, I was always afraid of going into a dark room because my mind painted a picture of a monster hiding in the dark. Images in the dark, even as simple as a lamp stand or a chair, created a wrong representation of a monster or someone hiding in the dark to get me. I don't know where kids get this idea of monsters under their beds, but it's probably safe to say most kids think that way. Of course, it was simply an illusion, a negative imagination that somehow got into my head.

On one occasion, an umbrella looked like a rifle-gun hanging on the wall in the dark. On another occasion, a pillow was on the floor in the dark, looking like a lifeless human. But as soon as the light was turned on, everything in the dark that had a false representation appearing real was exposed and revealed to be unreal, so my fear and worry immediately diminished.

Someone came up with this clever acronym for 'FEAR':

False

Evidence

Appearing

Real

You see, most of the things we worry about often come from the negativity and junk we fill our heads with from TV, books, posters, films, and social media (listening to other people's negative perspectives and misinformation). We worry because the enemy paints us a picture of failure in our darkest moments and a picture of our inadequacies and weaknesses during the most vulnerable times of our lives.

If the enemy can get you to believe a false shadow or a picture of something in your head that isn't real, he can victimize you with eternal pain: hopelessness, fear, and worry. When you are vulnerable, you will be robbed of your eternal joy. The Bible says in Ecclesiastes 5:3:

> *"A dream comes when there are many cares and many words mark the speech of a fool."*

The prophet Isaiah alluded to this simple truth of how we can keep our minds clear and free from negative-painted images that disrupt our peace and create fear in us in Isaiah 26:3:

> *"You will keep in perfect peace those whose minds are steadfast because they trust in you."*

Logic and Reason

All logic and reasoning take place in our heads. Reasoning in psychology is **the faculty or process of drawing logical inferences**. According to German philosopher Immanuel Kant, reasoning is *the* **power of synthesizing into unity utilizing comprehensive principles, the concepts provided by the intellect.**[8]

Perhaps we can say that the psychology of reasoning studies how people think things through or draw conclusions to solve problems and make decisions. It does overlap with philosophy, linguistics, cognitive science, artificial intelligence, logic, and probability theory.

Reasoning opposes sensation, feeling, perception and desire as the faculty by which fundamental truths are intuitively apprehended. Aristotle described reasoning as a part of human nature. He believed that humans should live 'politically,' meaning in communities about the size and type of a small city-state. We react with our emotions, but the daily wild thoughts in our heads are the driving force behind most of our daily actions. If we can control the urge to act upon the thoughts in our heads before we reason them through, then those negative actions won't stand a chance of coming to fruition.

The Power of Imagination

The word imagination comes from the Latin verb *imaginari*, meaning to picture oneself. This root definition of the word indicates the self-reflexive property of imagination, emphasizing imagination as a private sphere.

---

8   J., B. R. M., T., E. J. S. B., & Newstead, S. E. (2019). Human reasoning: The psychology of deduction. Psychology Press.

However, the *Oxford English Dictionary* defines imagination as the "act or power of forming a mental image of something not present to the senses or never before wholly perceived in reality." Said differently, imagination is the ability to create pictures in your mind of things that don't exist or that you've never seen or heard of before.

Imagination has its negative and positive side in the sense that it can be used to create, invent, and imagine good things happening in your future or envision the bad, the ugly and the worse coming your way. Oftentimes, our imagination preplays our future while our memories replay our past. If we fail to let go of our worst memories by constantly dwelling on them, they will eventually rob us of the ability to use our imagination to create a great future. We learn how to be what we dwell on most and forget that anything else is possible.

It is impossible to imagine a great future if you can't move beyond your awful, dreadful memories filled with fear, shame, and disappointment.

We live in a day and age where our imagination runs wild. The news and social media constantly bombard us… both are known for imparting misinformation, shaping our culture, and affecting our thoughts. The information transmitted through these various platforms creates images in our heads that often impair our functionality, causing us great harm and emotional and psychological instability. For instance, if I go to bed right after watching a two-hour horror movie, I tend to have nightmares, frightening dreams and sleepless nights because some of the scenes in the movie get stuck in my subconscious mind.

The subconscious mind only knows what you tell it. So, watching a horror movie or some disaster on the news can stick with you because you watched it with some emotion. The emotion behind it gave it power in your mind. Someone else might watch that same horror movie and laugh because they believe it's unlikely to happen. Their subconscious mind believes it's unlikely to happen.

Romans 12:2:

"Do not conform any longer to the pattern of this world, but be transformed by the renewing of your mind."

When you interpret life through the lens of God's Word rather than through your experience, woundedness, trauma, preferences, or the opinions of others, you won't be vulnerable; you'll be armed against false doctrines and misinformation.

The Law of Attraction

According to the Law of Attraction, how we think does affect our actions, behavior, and attitude. Many Christians believe this goes against God's will because you rely on your own power, not God's. I believe it goes along perfectly with God's will.

The *"ordinances of heaven and earth"* (Jeremiah 33:25), or what people call the Laws of the Universe or the Laws of Nature, are imminent, infallible laws that govern our universe, the universe God created.

If you think a certain way, you will act and behave a certain way. Thoughts become things. First, we have a thought. If we focus on that thought, we behave or act according to that thought, and then our lifestyle follows how we think and act. This can work for or against you, depending on what thoughts you focus on.

How we think is a force of attraction in itself. We attract certain personalities into our sphere based on the energy we put out. Our energy can influence others, and conversely, their energy affects us. Have you heard of good vibes or bad vibes? That's the physical vibration or energy put out by someone.

Based on our thought patterns, we can attract certain people… negative or positive. For example, business-minded people tend to attract other business-minded people, while pessimistic people attract their likes. As the saying goes, birds of the same feather flock together. Here's a simple analogy: If you decide you want to buy a certain type of car, you'll begin to see that model everywhere. Why? Because it's something you want, something you've been focusing on. It's the same with attracting people and opportunities. If you're looking for something in particular and are open to receiving it, you'll begin to see opportunities you might not have noticed before.

Begin to use the power of your mind to set in motion an environment that will aid you to flourish and prosper… an environment that will attract the right kind of people and opportunities.

The Thought Police

The mind is a powerful tool. It can be a terrible ground that produces streams of images that could cripple our ability to think clearly, act positively and believe affirmatively. These streams of images—the negative self-talk we subject ourselves to—could include a poor self-image, images of defeat, past failed relationships, hurts and disappointments, a mentality of lack… and so on.

John 10:10 says, *"The thief comes only to steal and kill and destroy."*

The negative images planted in your mind come from this thief in an attempt to diminish you; they do not come from God.

Psalm 23:5:

"My cup overflows…"

Deuteronomy 28:11:

"The Lord will grant you abundant prosperity..."

The Law of Abundance states that there is an unlimited amount of everything for everyone. There is no lack. It will never run out. And this is also in accordance with God's law.

When you align yourself with this principle, your belief that there just isn't enough to go around will fade.

But too often, the Thought Police come in and place restrictions, telling us we can't have that. These negative thought patterns can be broken into five categories that collectively cover almost everything in our lives.

- Health: fitness, weight, disease, physical self-image

- Dollars: investments, savings, spending, anything relating to money

- Business: career, job, school, volunteer work

- Relationships: family, friends, relatives, associates, neighbors, social

- Pleasure: travel, social, leisure, luxuries

God wants to give you the good things you deserve, but you have a limited worldview because of your past experiences, which is blocking your ability to receive.

You may be telling yourself that you want something, but your subconscious remembers all the times you didn't get it, whatever *it* is. It replays those same thoughts and experiences over and over.

The magic is you can substitute new thoughts that will work in the same way: thoughts of success and experiences that the mind thinks are real even though they haven't happened yet.

What do you think about it? And more importantly, *how* do you think about it?

Begin to say things like, "Oh, I'd like to do that," instead of, "I can't do that."

Always turn negatives into positives because the subconscious mind doesn't hear negatives. It only hears the root of the thought. So "I'm afraid of drowning" becomes "drowning." "I don't want to be broke anymore" becomes "broke."

Envision yourself being that person, doing or being what you want to be!

In extreme cases where you are afraid of drowning, just stay away from the water. But being broke can be turned around to "I have money coming in all the time." Don't use phrases like "I'm not broke" or "I'll never be broke again" because you're still saying "broke."

If you do that enough, your subconscious mind will believe it, your behaviors will change, and you'll begin to "attract" those things you desire. In other words, you'll be receptive and open to recognizing and receiving God's gifts for you.

Any unhappiness you experience is caused by denying the present and attaching importance to the past and the future. This is where all the negative self-talk comes from.

The subconscious mind sees life in movies. It doesn't know what's real. That's why you're terrified when you walk to your car in the dark after seeing a scary movie. Your subconscious mind is telling you to be afraid. Why? Because it's still watching the movie.

You need to be an observer of your thoughts.

The Thought Police are working for or against you, whether you realize it or not.

You don't believe there's enough to go around.

You don't believe you can lose weight and keep it off this time.

You don't believe you can land that client or close that sale.

You don't believe you're pretty, smart, talented, and lucky enough to deserve the privilege of the few who 'have it all.'

This is referred to as a scarcity mindset.

But God and His Laws work equally for everyone.

You haven't yet recognized that by *not* focusing your energy and consciousness on what you *want* to become, you have become the random manifestation of all the energy you've experienced, which has developed into your current perspective.

You have subconsciously put out to the world everything you believe about the way things are—that there is a lack and not enough to go around—and this is what you've received.

Change what you put out, and you will change what you get back.

Rather than allowing yourself to be a victim of your past negative experiences, being merely a byproduct of your wrongly-conditioned thinking, consciously create your reality. The thoughts you have exist because you gave them life. Now they police everything you do. This is powerful stuff.

Defeating negative self-talk is as simple as replacing it with positive thoughts and actions. Begin by putting yourself in a positive environment.

> Walk in the park or a beautiful setting. Many office plazas are stunning.
>
> Read an uplifting book; read the Bible.
>
> Visit a museum where the art is inspiring.
>
> Take in an open-air concert or buy yourself a headset to listen to nice music as you walk or run.
>
> Go to a seminar or take a class in something you like; try something new!

Anything you can do to put yourself around positive people and environments will be beneficial. And while you're there, redirect your thoughts away from your negative image and self-talk to the positivity around you.

Just Breathe

Learning to exhale to unclog your mind and inhale the peace of God's love in every situation and circumstance is therapeutic for your mind, body, and soul. However, people sometimes take the alternative route of hiding their pain in all addictions.

Research shows that our failure to confront our negative emotional roller coaster, secret fears, anxiety, the void and the emptiness that we feel on the inside tends to be the breeding ground for substance abuse, alcohol addiction, and suicidal thoughts. Remember, the energy you give out is the energy you get back. So, in the quest to fill a void and deal with our negative energy or paranoiac behavior, we might be prone to exploring and leaning on temporary solutions to numb our pain rather than going deep down to the root to seek a more permanent solution and a definitive cure.

Again, take a breather from your stressful life or whatever is causing your pain. Seek out positive experiences. Sometimes, just experiencing something new, like taking an art class, can open your perspective of the world.

Recognizing Triggers

Recognizing what triggers anxiety, worry, panic attacks and fear in you could pose a great challenge. But these emotional paralysis or attacks could be traced to one thing leading to another. The following highlights are a few trigger agents:

- Lack of rest and sleep

- Over-thinking or over-analyzing

- Insecurity

- Bad and negative news or information received

- Trying to juggle too many things at the same time— having too much on your plate

- Unorganized lifestyle; feeling constantly harried

- An overbearing attitude—dwelling on the past and refusing to let go

Try to observe yourself from the outside in. When something triggers you, it may be difficult not to react, but if you do, tough it out until you calm down. Then try to pinpoint what caused the reaction, what triggered you. By doing this, you can become more aware of this trigger the next time it happens, and perhaps you can deal with it better because you can see it for what it is: just a trigger.

Live | Laugh | Love

To be able to overcome your emotional paralysis brought on by fear, anxiety, worry and panic attacks, you have to make a conscious effort to reprogram and rewire your mind and your emotions to live a little… laugh a little… and love a little. Researchers from Finland and the United Kingdom found that social laughter triggers the release of endorphins and dopamine, often called feel-good hormones. Endorphins are peptides that interact with opioid receptors in the brain to help relieve pain and trigger feelings of pleasure. The study also revealed that the more opioid receptors people have in the brain region associated with the processing of emotions, the more they engage in social laughter.

Over the years in my personal life, I have come to find out that the more I consciously program my mind and my emotions to live well despite life challenges, laugh in the midst of my pain and turmoil, and pray my way through disappointments and heartbreaks, the more empowered I become to deal with my emotional paralysis and take full control of my situation.

Remember, there are physiological changes that occur in the body due to both positive and negative thinking. That's why stress causes illness. You can turn it around by intentionally turning your thoughts into positive things. Make them up if you have to. God gave us an imagination for a reason!

CHAPTER FIVE

THE MEDICAL, PSYCHOLOGICAL & EMOTIONAL EFFECTS OF FEAR, WORRY & ANXIETY

Fight or Flight: The Body's Response to Stress

In looking at the causes of stress, remember that your brain comes hard-wired with an alarm system for your protection. The fight or flight response at the core of our brain is a survival mechanism, something left over from the days when man had to deal with stressful situations like fighting wild animals with handmade weapons. He could either fight the animal or run from it. He didn't have to think about natural health. It just came… well, naturally.

During times of increased stress, the liver and pancreas dump enormous amounts of sugar and insulin into the bloodstream in response to the emergency. This served the caveman well. He was pumped up to fight or run, and whatever he chose to do, he used this excess sugar.

When we face an emergency or dangerous situation, muscle tension, breathing, and heart rate increase, blood races to the heart and brain from other organs, oxygen increases in the brain, and blood sugar level rises, adrenaline, cortisol, and other hormones are released.

Unfortunately, the nonstop stress of modern living means that our alarm system rarely shuts off. Recent developments from WebMD show that worrying can bring about physical illness. Chronic worry and emotional stress can trigger a host of health problems. The body responds to physical and mental stressors as it does to injuries, electric shock, and harmful environmental toxic substances. The release of stress hormones by the body's sympathetic nervous system goes unchecked and unused. There is no fire to put out, no bear to kill, no tribes to fight, and nothing to use up the cortisol and adrenaline that then contribute to high blood pressure, heart disease, obesity, and diabetes, and it will have a major effect on longevity. These hormones also boost blood sugar levels and ***triglycerides*** [blood fats].

Today, because we have no outlet for these excesses, they're stored in the fat cells, usually in the abdomen. Fat is inherently inflammatory and triggers more stress. And it's just as often not the threat that causes stress but the perception of the stressor or threat, suggesting that most modern stress is self-induced.

These hormones, when left unchecked, also cause physical reactions such as:

- difficulty swallowing

- dizziness

- dry mouth

- fast heartbeat

- fatigue

- headaches

- inability to concentrate

- irritability

- muscle tension

- nausea

- nervous energy

- shortness of breath

- trembling and twitching

Fear and worry have a way of psychologically and emotionally traumatizing and trapping you in a world of the unknown and unknowable, and this uncertainty stresses us out. The longer we give ourselves to excessive fear and worry, the more emotionally destabilized we become because worry and fear drain confidence and the desire to believe and become.

You will never outperform your confidence and the self-portrait that you have of yourself.

There comes a time in your life when you will have to accept these possible convictions or evaluations of yourself:

what you think about yourself

what others think about you

what satan (your enemy) thinks about you

what God thinks about you

Whenever people focus more on a problem than the solution, they become emotionally and psychologically derailed and disturbed, failing to see past their present predicament.

Understanding Emotional Responses and the Effects of Worry, Fear and Anxiety

Worry, fear, and anxiety are all human emotional responses to a likely event or circumstance in the past, present or future. They all get triggered by similar brain processes and have similar psychological and behavioral reactions. Most recent research reveals that two separate pathways in the brain can create anxiety. One part begins in the cerebral cortex, the part of the brain that involves our perceptions and thoughts. The other part is the amygdala, which is responsible for the ancient fight or flight response. However, unlike worry and anxiety, fear is always associated with a present occurrence or an identifiable threat, like when we are in trouble. For example, when an intruder breaks into our home. On the other hand, we feel anxiety when we worry about the unknown, when we are under stress due to trying to meet a deadline or when it is late at night. We haven't heard from a son or daughter who had left home earlier with friends without leaving a note or calling to let the family know his or her whereabouts.

> **Anxiety also gets a hold of us when our imagination begins to run wild about what could be.**

The more we logically try to figure out what lies ahead, the more worry arises. Worry frequently paints us a picture of the worst that could happen. It also robs us of the opportunity to think about things going right instead of going wrong.

> **Worry creates emotional paralysis that challenges our ability and creativity to devise a way out of our misery and captivity.**

Reality-Based Worry

Reality-based worry always occurs when we are overcome by thinking about what we forgot to do, for example, or wondering what harm could occur due to our actions or inaction. This reality could often worry us to death, even though it is simply a thought that might not be true. For example, leaving the gas station and unsure if you replaced the gas cap. This worry-thought will eventually make you pull over and check the gas cap. However, to determine if your worry is a reality-based worry-thought, it must be a worrythought that you can do something about, something you have control over.

Anxiety Under Control

There are ways you can ease your anxiety and get it under control. Organizing self-care is of utmost importance. I cannot overemphasize ensuring you are getting enough rest and eating well—because what we eat can influence our state of mind and anxiety levels.

- Avoid eating lots of sugar; read labels. There is hidden sugar in many packaged products.

- Limit caffeine and nicotine. These are catalysts for anxiety.

- Create a strategy to decrease pressure and practice more unwinding in your life. This could be through physical exercise, breathing activities, or other treatments like getting a massage or using essential oils for healing.

- Designate work. If you're overworked, it may be worth spending money on a housekeeper one day a week to relieve some of the household duties.

- Many have discovered the power of yoga, meditation and reflection to be most effective in decreasing pressure.

Minimizing Panic Attacks

Engaging yourself with a few of these exercises could help you cope better when panic attacks strike:

Close your eyes and attempt to concentrate on your breath. Follow the air flowing; visualize your breath as it goes in and out. This activity will let you centre and quiet your psyche during panic attacks. Don't try to "control" your breathing. Simply "watch it" as it flows; eventually, it will slow down.

Always recognize the attack as it occurs. Hence, this will encourage you to adapt to and acknowledge the truth of the occasion—it will also kill the intensity of the panic attack. During an attack, always try to relax, calm yourself down and be mindful of what your body and brain are doing at that very moment.

Mental focus, humane treatment, and unwinding are recommended when panic attacks become extremely prevalent. An in-depth treatment may require a prescription. Consult your primary care physician for treatment.

The Addiction Response

People respond emotionally differently when dealing with worry, fear and anxiety. Some will immediately turn to drugs, alcohol, sex, or gluttony or develop other eating disorders such as anorexia. Some may even resort to excessive shopping as a way out or gambling… all to fill an empty void.

They say addiction is the disease that makes you too selfish to see the havoc you created or care about the people whose lives you have shattered. The addiction response will not eradicate your worry, anxiety or fear; it only numbs your emotional response to pain. Russell Brand has this to say about addiction: "The priority of any addict is to anaesthetize the pain of living, to ease the passage of day with some purchased relief."

Your recovery from addiction must come first so that everything you love in life does not come last. And the only way to stay recovered is to create a life more rewarding than the one you are trying to leave behind.

Breaking Old Habits and Patterns

First and foremost, acknowledging that you have a habit you'd like to break is vital. Consider how the habit alters or affects your life, and accept that you'd like to change this. It starts with a dream and the passion to achieve something worthwhile.

Next comes the commitment to carry out the tasks. Be realistic, as it is going to take some extra energy. Something must be given up. Be certain not to let family and friends sabotage your plans. You have your priorities, so stick with them. Often, getting started is the hardest step. You must commit to realizing sacrifice and establish priorities to meet your goal. Bad habits are easy to get into but can be hard to eliminate. There must be a specific but realistic goal. If you think you can do it, you can achieve it. Make a detailed plan or set of tasks to establish sub-goals. Ask yourself what must be done and what habits need to be developed and sustained to ensure you reach the goal.

If I were asked to give two words to ensure success, they would be "correct habits." I say correct habits because knowing, undergoing the correct training, and adopting the correct daily diet and exercise will help contribute to a healthy lifestyle. A lack of good long-term habits will mean a lack of success. You must do the right task to get the right result.

It's been proven that it takes an average of thirty days to form any habit before it forms us. The habits that we form in response to our emotional state of worry, fear and anxiety eventually, in the long run, become detrimental to our healing or recovery process, especially when those habits are hard to break free from. For example, people who get hooked on cigarettes/nicotine or marijuana because of stress, anxiety or worry tend to find it more difficult to respond to medical or other forms of therapy because of their dependency upon the use of these substances.

Research suggests that sometimes, our environment can cue us to perform certain behaviors, even if we're actively trying to stop. Find a way to change your scenery and see if your bad habit becomes less tempting. For instance, if you like to smoke out on your patio, remove the chair you sit in and replace it with a plant. If you tend to overeat at the same location at the dining room table, move to a different seat or rearrange your furniture such that you're facing a different direction than usual when you eat. Subtle environmental changes can lessen tempting triggers and force your mind to reassess what's happening.

Limit your interactions with people who encourage your bad habits. If your bad habit takes place in an environment that you can't alter, like your place of work, then try changing the social configuration of your habit. For instance, if you smoke on breaks with a group of coworkers, start timing your break differently so that you're not tempted to join the fray and light up. Your social life might change, but your health will improve.

CHAPTER SIX

THE LIES THAT WORRY PRODUCES

1 Peter 5:7 says:

> *"Cast all your anxiety on him because he cares for you."*

Lie #1: Anxiety

So, one of the lies that worry produces is Anxiety. As I mentioned in the previous chapter, anxiety comprises worry, nervousness and a feeling or sense of uneasiness. It is typically about an imminent event or something with an uncertain outcome.

Anxiety is also having a preconceived notion of what could go wrong. It could include panic attacks, a false anticipation of things not working out well, or things going sideways. Said differently, Anxiety anticipates the worst with little hope for the best. This is called *learned helplessness*. It's a reaction to situations we can't control or think we can't.

Our anxiety sometimes reveals our inability and failure to trust the process God takes us through before a manifestation or the tangibility of the desired miracles in our lives.

Lie # 2: Insecurity

Another lie that worry produces is a feeling of insecurity. Insecurity is a strong negative emotion that robs you of your hope for a future and the ability to see beyond. The feeling of insecurity always makes you need to compare yourself to others. The byproduct of this act creates in you a sense of inadequacy… forgetting that no two humans are created with the same abilities. Even our DNA is different. By focusing on what others think you are missing or lacking in your life, you fail to recognize your God-given talent and purpose.

Insecurity may also lead to envy and jealousy. Envy and jealousy are primitive ways of expressing frustration with inadequacy. Redirecting these negative emotions will challenge you to undertake more self-education, which will enable you to become a master of your craft and giftings. You gain the confidence to overcome your insecurities by improving your gifts, talents, and abilities.

Lie #3: Uncertainty

Another lie that worry produces is uncertainty. This produces a lack of peace and causes the absence of all sensitivity. The moment we begin to worry, just because we are unsure of what tomorrow may bring, we lose all sensitivity and the ability to recognize the fact that, though we might not know what tomorrow holds, we have today before us that we must endeavor to maximize, make the best out of, and live it to its fullest. You can transfer the attitude of gratitude for this day into your tomorrow.

> **How you live your today will determine how you live your tomorrow.**

Lie #4 Hopelessness

The feeling that the sun will never shine again—I am done—is another result of worry. This is a trap many people fall into, especially when pressure begins to mount up and the situation becomes hopeless.

Dr. Mike Murdock said in one of his writings, "Sometimes you can be so closed up or engulfed by your mountain that you can't see the trees around. In our darkest moments of despair, we tend to lose sight of being able to see the light of day again someday. In that moment of insurmountable chaos and adversity, it always feels like an eternity, a living hell on earth."

Lie #5: Wishful Thinking

A life of worry always brings many wishes along with it. When we are submerged in an ocean of predicaments, a parade of uncertainty and hopelessness, these are some of the wishes that come to mind:

> I wish I had the right connections or knew the right people
>
> I wish life weren't so unfair
>
> I wish I could have done things differently
>
> I wish I were born into a wealthy family or born on the other side of the world, of a different race or ethnicity
>
> I wish I had a college degree
>
> I wish I married Mr. Right or Mrs. Right
>
> I wish I could move the hand of God faster

I wish I were taller, prettier or more handsome

I wish I were an only child

I wish I had more, more, more…

Lie #6: Self-Pity

Whenever life kicks us so hard and pushes our backs against the wall, we can't, in our wildest dreams, imagine anyone else going through what we are going through. We immediately resolve to despair. "Nobody knows the trouble I've seen; nobody knows my sorrow…" is a line from a Negro spiritual, but it perfectly sums up how we feel when we isolate ourselves and our troubles. We unequivocally validate our problem or trouble to be far worse than anyone else's could be.

Here's something for your encouragement… a biblical admonition by the apostle Paul, whom many believed to have written most of the New Testament.

1 Corinthians 10:13 (The Message Bible Translation):

"No test or temptation that comes your way is beyond the course of what others have had to face. All you need to remember is that God will never let you down; he'll never let you be pushed past your limit; he'll always be there to help you overcome it."

Lie # 7: Imagining the negative things that be not as though they were

Your imagination is a powerful tool. It preplays the future things that haven't happened yet. On the other hand, your memory replays the past things that have already happened.

Your imagination and memory can be used positively and most productively to create momentum for the future (imagination) or draw energy, inspiration and testimony from past victory (memory).

When David faced his enemy on the battlefield… the 9foot-tall giant named Goliath, he consulted his memory to replay past victories of defeating the bear and the lion. He went further to enumerate the fact that the same method and God that delivered him from the bear and the lion was able to deliver him from the uncircumcised Philistine.

1 Samuel 17:34-37:

> "But David said to Saul, "Your servant has been keeping his father's sheep. When a lion or a bear came and carried off a sheep from the flock, I went after it, struck it and rescued the sheep from its mouth. When it turned on me, I seized it by its hair, struck it and killed it. Your servant has killed both the lion and the bear; this uncircumcised Philistine will be like one of them, because he has defied the armies of the living God. The Lord who rescued me from the paw of the lion and the paw of the bear will rescue me from the hand of this Philistine."

Saul told David, *"Go, and the Lord be with you."*

However, a repressed, painful and hurtful memory, or imagining all the negative things that are not as they were, are some of the lies that worry produces in us. This act could be detrimental to our mental well-being.

Lie #8: It wasn't meant to be

Has your heart ever been ripped apart and your hope destroyed? In moments like this, you wish it never happened. Maybe you've been through a divorce, a break up with your girlfriend or boyfriend, or maybe you've been let go from a job that you have put many years into, and now you feel like Job in the Bible who lost it all, and eventually cursed the day he was born.

Whenever life hits us terribly, most people begin to live with the self-consolation that "maybe it wasn't meant to be." The job wasn't meant for them, and the relationship wasn't meant to last longer. The marriage was supposed to end in separation or divorce… yada, yada, yada.

Truth be told, when you start to believe these lies, you'll start to worry unnecessarily. This will destroy you emotionally and incapacitate you physically and mentally so much that it will keep you from reaching for more.

CHAPTER SEVEN

THE ANTIDOTE | CURE FOR WORRY

Replace Your Worries With Worship!!!!

To worry is to believe the enemy's lies, but to worship is to exalt and magnify the highest God over your situation and circumstances. Worship helps you take your mind off the situation and helps you focus it on the one who can calm every raging storm in your life. In doing so, you gain insight delivered through that calm. Therefore, one of the antidotes or cures for worry I recommend is *worship*.

When we worship and bask in God's presence, a sense of reassurance floods our minds and souls… a sense of peace that reinforces a total trust and dependency upon God's promises. God's presence always creates a spiritual harbor for us when we encounter the storms and devastation that life brings. His presence becomes a life jacket for our covering and protection when the hurricanes and the winds of chaos blow through our minds' doors and windows.

When we worship God… we worship him for who he is.

When we praise him… we are praising and thanking him for what he has done.

If there was one Bible character who knew what it meant to praise and worship our God, it is David, the psalmist! Hear his heart in this favorite passage of Psalms.

Psalm 103:1-5:

"Praise the Lord, my soul; all my inmost being, praise his holy name. Praise the Lord, my soul, and forget not all his benefits who forgives all your sins and heals all your diseases, who redeems your life from the pit and crowns you with love and compassion, who satisfies your desires with good things so that your youth is renewed like the eagle's."

Psalm 100:1-4

"Shout for joy to the Lord, all the earth. Worship the Lord with gladness; come before him with joyful songs. Know that the Lord is God. It is he who made us, and we are His; We are His people, the sheep of his pasture."

"Enter his gates with thanksgiving and his courts with praise; give thanks to him and praise his name."

Proverbs 17:22 also tells us:

"A cheerful heart is good medicine, but a crushed spirit dries up the bones."

The King James Version uses the word *merry*, which means to be in a state of being cheerful and lively.

Recent studies show that music and certain sounds can change or impact a person's mood. Slow funeral procession songs can fill an auditorium with sadness, gloom and sorrow. At the same time, upbeat songs have a way of creating a lively vibe in any environment. Most young adult clothing stores or local gyms understand this concept. That's why they play upbeat songs to set the right atmosphere, to motivate and create a sense of urgency to keep you shopping or burning those calories non-stop. Worship songs impact and calm a fearful and worried spirit because the sound of worship tends to usher in the presence of God.

A Steadfast Heart on God's Promises and Provision

Sometimes, it pays to go back to the word of God and do an in-depth study of what his promises are for us, especially when we find ourselves in a very low place in our lives. Some will refer to this low place as being in the valley. Psalm 37 is a good one to pay attention to when the going gets rough and tough, and we can't seem to find the strength to hold on—to get through and to keep going in a positive direction.

Psalm 37:1-7:

> *"Do not fret because of those who are evil or be envious of those who do wrong; for like the grass, they will soon wither; like green plants, they will soon die away."*

> *"Trust in the Lord and do good; dwell in the land and enjoy safe pasture. Take delight in the Lord, and he will give you the desires of your heart. Commit your way to the Lord; trust in him, and he will do this: He will make your righteous reward shine like the dawn, your vindication like the noonday sun."*

> *"Be still before the Lord and wait patiently for him; do not fret when people succeed in their ways or carry out their wicked schemes."*

The Spiritual Law of Recognition

In walking in the Spiritual Law of Recognition, it's important to remember that what you *fail to recognize, place value on,* or *hold up in high esteem* will stop working for you. The name of Jesus will only work for you if you believe it can break yokes and bondages off your life and calm every raging storm.

This goes back to your most focused thoughts. What you think about most will be what appears to you regardless of what it is. When you focus your heart and mind on His laws, you will receive all the gifts promised to you in kind. But you must be diligent in this. It's okay to ask for what you want. When you pray, ask. In my humble opinion, it's not enough to say, "Lord, send me what is mine." This is a vague, though valid, prayer. However, if you add specifically what you need, you might be surprised at how much you receive.

So walking in the Law of Recognition, who we are in Christ, and how much more valuable we are to him than the birds of the air or the lilies of the field, who get cared for without worrying, is a spiritual remedy for gaining victory over your fear, your worry, and the uncertainties that life brings. Our Lord and Savior gave his disciples this warning in the gospel of Matthew 6:26-27.

Matthew 6:26-27:

> *"Look at the birds of the air; they do not sow or reap or store away in barns, and yet your heavenly Father feeds them. Are you not much more valuable than they? Can any one of you by worrying add a single hour to your life?"*

This Law of Recognition can also apply to our new birth in Christ. Our new birth in Christ gives us the right and access to God to lay our petition and burdens down at his feet. Old ways and things that made us worry have been done away with, and all things have been made new. The recognition of this simple spiritual law should alleviate our worry and anxiety. Our confidence should be restored. But many Christians still cling to the worry that is bringing them down.

The Apostle Paul alluded to this Spiritual Law of Recognition in his letter to the Corinthian church.

2 Corinthians 5:17:

"Therefore, if anyone is in Christ, he is a new creation; old things have passed away; behold, all things have become new."

Chances, Choices, and Changes

Life will always give you more than a million reasons to worry if you let it. But life also gives us choices. Some people go through life seeing things through a glass of pessimism, while others go through life seeing things through a glass of optimism. No matter what you have been dealt with in life, your perception, your reaction, and how you choose to see things in every life's circumstances is totally up to you; it's a matter of choice.

The three Cs of life are **CHANCES, CHOICES,** *and* **CHANGES.**

If you do not make the *choice* to take a *chance* in life, a *change* will never come.

Choosing to see the brighter side of things in a downwardspiraling negative world sets you apart from the majority. The ability to always look beyond what is to what shall be is the difference between letting the trajectory of your present circumstances define your tomorrow and future aspirations. Choose to use the lessons you've learned along the way as a springboard to launch you into the deep for innovation and creativity.

Refuse the temptation of trying to live up to people's expectations. This is a choice. Trying to live up to other people's expectations is like trying to live your life under the scrutiny and judgment of people's opinion of you; don't do it. It will wear you out. Opinions, they say, are like noses, and everyone has one.

Winston Churchill made this observation:

> "When we are in our twenties, we wonder what people think about us; when we are in our forties, we stop worrying much about what other people think about us; and when we get to our sixties, we realize that no one was thinking about us."

Realizing that everyone falls short will liberate you from worrying and trying to measure up. You can only "measure up" to your best potential, not the one someone else has dictated.

Refuse the trap of letting past negative experiences influence you today. This is a choice. Whenever life pulls you back into a familiar situation that you have encountered before, once upon a time, instead of worrying and panicking, simply remember how you got over it before and be convinced that this, too, shall pass. If God pulled you through before, he'd pull you through again; if he did it before, he'd do it again. A songwriter says, "Just take a look at where you are now and where you've been."…God will always come through for you with his grace and strength to pull you through.

Let your inner peace guide you. This is a choice! Occasionally, we all experience a sense of peace and serenity within our souls.

But to get back to that place, we need to stop worrying! There is no worry in peace, nor peace in worry!

The Bible talks about the peace that passes all understanding in the book of Philippians.

Philippians 4:6-7:

> *"Do not be anxious about anything, but in every situation, by prayer and petition, with thanksgiving, present your requests to God. And the peace of God, which transcends all understanding, will guard your hearts and your minds in Christ Jesus."*

The Hebrew word for peace is *shalom*. It means a sense of placidity, calmness, tranquility and ease… the absence of chaos and peace amid uncertainty. Over the years, I have learned that this kind of peace sometimes indicates that everything will be alright, even though we can't figure out how it will all come together.

Focus on the end result. This is a choice. Focusing on the end result rather than dwelling on the current prevailing circumstances gives us a sense of hope and confidence for what lies ahead. It helps us to take the steps necessary to resolve the problem. We are reminded in the book of Ecclesiastes with these words:

Ecclesiastes 7:8:

> *"The end of a matter is better than its beginning, and patience is better than pride."*

Focusing on the end result always helps you go through the process without fainting, becoming weary or losing sight along the way.

Avoid the deadline pressure. This is a choice! Give yourself the space and time for things to unfold. We all know that the deadline pressure is an adrenaline elevator. Some people function well under pressure, but it can also depend on the circumstances. The pressure of having a deadline, if not managed effectively, can cause stress that affects us mentally and physiologically.

Planning well will help you avoid most of the pressure and tension that comes with having deadlines, but sometimes, things just don't go as planned. If the pressure is in your personal life—you planned on getting certain things done over the weekend, but life got in the way—you can make adjustments. But most deadline pressure comes in the form of job expectations.

As soon as you realize there's a problem, that you're not going to meet your deadline, inform your manager your boss, and let that person know. They will likely help you devise a contingency plan or reset the deadline.

Refrain from negativity, anxiety, and anticipation. This is a choice! Anticipating the worst will lead you to unnecessary, endless worry, anxiety and frustration. You can't control the future, nor can you change the past. And often, you can't even control the present circumstances, but you can plan well and prepare adequately. Here's a biblical reference that could drive this point home.

Proverbs 22:29:

> *"Seest thou a man diligent in his business? He shall stand before kings; he shall not stand before mean men."*

I love the way Eugene Peterson translates this.

Don't Worry About It: Go to Bed

Proverbs 22:29–Message Bible translation:

*"Observe people who are good at their work; skilled
workers are always in demand and admired;
they don't take a backseat to anyone."*

In his wisdom in Proverbs 6:11, Solomon referred to the calm, lackadaisical attitude we humans tend to display. This negative, lazy attitude keeps us from moving toward any goal or vision.

Proverbs 6:6-11:

*"Go to the ant, you sluggard; consider its ways and be wise!
It has no commander, no overseer or ruler, yet it stores
its provisions in summer and gathers its food at harvest.
How long will you lie there, you sluggard? When will you
get up from your sleep? A little sleep, a little slumber, a
little folding of the hands to rest, and poverty will come
on you like a thief and scarcity like an armed man."*

In this text, Solomon uses the ant, one of the most productive insects known to us, to compare to humans (referred to here as sluggards). The ant's effectiveness and ability to plan are considered admirable.

I looked up the word sluggard. It simply means one who is lazy and sluggish. So, could it be that sometimes, due to our laziness in preparing and planning ahead, we create an endless parade of stress, anxiety and worry in our lives?

I have lived long enough to have learned this simple truth: that our failure to launch out early and give ourselves enough time and room for the unforeseen, the unfortunate and the unexpected delays that we may encounter along the way, could be the reason for all the drama and tension that ensues when our goals are not met the way we thought they would be, the way we expected them to, even though we haven't actually laid out a plan.

Becoming early birds in planning any project, goal, vision, or appointment could spare us from the heartache of rushing through these important aspects of life; we can easily avoid becoming the *last-minute dot com* person. Waiting till the last minute to embark upon a task is a recipe for anxiety. You'll worry about what could go wrong whenever you find yourself in this predicament. It is inevitable.

CHAPTER EIGHT

THE KEYS TO A RESTFUL SLEEP

A restful sleep always begins with a peaceful mind. The opposite is a medical term known as insomnia. According to WebMD, insomnia is a sleep disorder in which you have trouble falling or staying asleep. The condition can be transient (less than one week), short-term (acute insomnia), or chronic insomnia (long-term).

Depression and insomnia can be closely linked. People with insomnia may have a tenfold higher risk of developing depression than those with a good night's sleep. And among people with depression, seventy-five percent have trouble falling asleep or staying asleep. During the night, there are five stages of sleep that one can experience multiple times. During sleep, the body repairs itself, but if we are always in and out of sleep, we'll fall short of reaching the maximum capacity of every one of these stages, which can lead to inadequate or full restoration. Chemical restoration and repairs needed to fight off stress throughout the day will fall short. If this inadequate repair is kept up for long, the illness will eventually take hold.

Here are the stages of sleep (based on an analysis of brain activity during sleep, which showed distinct patterns that characterize each stage):

1. **Pre-stage 1**: Falling asleep: This is not a sleep stage; you should be able to fall asleep and stay asleep within 15 minutes of bed.

2. **Stage 1**: NREM (N1 – light sleep): N1 lasts 17 minutes. The body and brain activity start to slow down.

3. **Stage 2**: NREM (N2 – subdued sleep): temperature drops, eye movement stops, muscles relax. N2 lasts 10-25 minutes.

4. **Stage 3**: NREM (N3 – slow-wave sleep): critical to restorative sleep; contributes to insightful thinking, creativity, memory, and immune strength. N3 typically lasts 20-40 minutes.

5. **Stage 4**: REM (rapid eye movement sleep): begins about 90 minutes into sleep; brain activity increases to nearly the same level as awake. The body experiences atonia, or paralysis of the muscles, except for the eyes, heart, and respiratory muscles. REM is also critical to cognitive function, learning and creativity. Vivid dreaming occurs. REM can last from a few minutes early into sleep to an hour later.

Research shows that our body and mind need at least 6-8 hours of sleep to achieve its utmost rejuvenation. Too many sleepless nights can cause a lot of health issues. The sequence to a restful sleep starts with clearing your mind and laying aside every weight, worry, fear, and anxiety you have carried all day. We are admonished in Psalm 18:2 with these words:

> *"The Lord is my rock, my fortress and my deliverer;*
> *my God is my rock, in whom I take refuge, my shield*
> *and the horn of my salvation, my stronghold."*

Psalm 127:2 lets us know how God truly gives sleep to us.

> *"In vain, you rise early and stay up late, toiling for*
> *food to eat—for he grants sleep to those he loves."*

We have to get to a place in our lives where we realize the frailty of the human mind. Harboring junk, grudges and negativity, which, over time, become more like compound interest that catches up with us. And not in a good way. We have to learn to forgive quickly and worry less about things we can't change or control.

It's Time to Unwind

According to bodywork literature, unwinding is based on the simple principle of the body's ability for self-correction from mechanical disturbances. Tissues hold memories of trauma. The unwinding process allows the body to easily adjust to a new position. Though our body has a way of regenerating itself, over time, the wear and tear that our bodies undergo can take a huge toll on our physical, psychological and emotional well-being.

Re-Learning to Sleep

So, what can you do before bed to help your body unwind?

> **Turn the lights out** - Optometrists let us know that too many light rays in our eyes could create a fault of refraction, hence a distraction in achieving the right sleeping atmosphere or mood. I must admit that the slightest ray of light in my bedroom can keep me awake all night. However, if you must have lights on, a dim blue light could be a great alternative because it is softer and calmer to the eyes, unlike harsh white lights. Street lights or light coming from other houses often can't be turned off. Try using blackout blinds or eye covers to get the room dark.
>
> **The Amish Hour** - Having the TV on in the bedroom psychologically tells you that the day is not over, and good night kisses are not yet to be made. Practice what's called The

Amish Hour. Turn off all electronic devices at least one hour before bedtime. That includes phones, TVs, computers, tablets, headsets—all of it.

Create your lullabies - One of the keys to a restful sleep is eliminating every form of noise and creating an atmosphere of total quietness and calmness. After a long, stressful day of life's hustle and bustle, our soul longs for and deserves an absolute night of bliss to reset-refresh-rejuvenate and replenish.

For me, an instrumental worship song, a soulful spa instrumental sound, or even a Kenny G jazz instrumental does the magic of bringing total relaxation to my tired body aching joints and rocking my soul to sleep.

Pillows, mattresses, sheets & comforters - a physical therapist once told me that most people do not emphasize getting the right mattress to support their body or pillow to support their neck. A little investment in the right orthopedic mattress might not be a bad idea since our bed is where we return for rest and some pampering after a long day's work. Additionally, make sure your blankets are cozy to your taste. They should not be too heavy because the body's heat is up at night.

What else can you do?

Get sun – helps the body create serum 25 hydroxyvitamin D, promoting sleep.

Avoid alcohol and caffeine before bed – both are stimulants.

Maintain a sleep schedule – going to sleep and getting up simultaneously daily.

Eliminate noise – noise prevents the mind from relaxing.

Here are a few of my favorite biblical verses for a restful sleep:

Psalm 116:7:

> *"Return to your rest, my soul, for the Lord has been good to you."*

Psalm 4:8:

> *"In peace, I will lie down and sleep, for you alone, Lord, make me dwell in safety."*

Matthew 11:28-30:

> *"Come to me, all you who are weary and burdened, and I will give you rest. Take my yoke upon you and learn from me, for I am gentle and humble in heart, and you will find rest for your souls. For my yoke is easy and my burden is light."*

CHAPTER NINE

TOOLS FOR OVERCOMING WORRY, FEAR & ANXIETY

31 Daily Affirmations & Confessions

Daily affirmations and positive confessions definitely have their place in overcoming and dealing with our worry, fear and anxiety. Such affirmations and confessions can sometimes help rewire our brain and mindset, gravitating us towards emotional wholeness and confidence. Here are some of my favorite affirmations, and please be aware that this list is inexhaustible.

1. I have control over my anxiety
2. I do not fear the worst; I anticipate the best
3. I choose to worry less and become more hopeful
4. I am not afraid; I am confident and brave
5. My past is behind me; my future is ahead of me
6. I firmly believe that all things will work out for my good
7. I will not let my present circumstances dictate the outcome of my destiny

8. I am a very determined and driven individual

9. I am not wired to live a worried life

10. I am anxious for nothing

11. I live a victorious and triumphant life

12. I walk in divine health and prosperity

13. I am mentally and emotionally sound and vibrant

14. I choose to live life beyond the limit

15. I am thriving and winning both in my relationships and finances

16. I choose to forgive others because I have been forgiven

17. I am determined to let go of every weight and emotional paralysis that holds me bound

18. I choose to give thanks and have a grateful heart

19. I will not stop learning and growing to improve myself 20.

20. I refuse to play the blame game; instead, I seek reconciliation rather than retaliation

21. Giving up is not an option for me—holding on and moving forward is what I strive for

22. I refuse to procrastinate on my visions and dreams—I choose to be proactive

23. I'll always give my 100% to what I do

24. I am a finisher; I am not a half-way individual—I choose to see things to the end

25. I choose to be open-minded, to explore new heights and horizons, and not become skeptical

26. I refuse to let other people's opinions define me

27. I am not perfect, but I am committed

28. I will not let my vulnerability blindfold me to life's reality

29. I'll be careful of who I allow into my space and circle of influence—because bad company corrupts good manners

30. I won't get myself worked up over people I can't seem to figure out or whose ways I don't understand

31. I refused to be paranoid over life's illusions

When these daily affirmations and confessions become part of your vocabulary, they will reset, renew, and brainwash your mind from all the negativity. Psychologists observe that what we meditate on and repeatedly say to ourselves influences our minds and actions. What we say and believe about ourselves also has a way of projecting for us a better self-image.

20 Biblical Texts to Help You Overcome

1. Joshua 1:9

"Have I not commanded you? Be strong and courageous. Do not be afraid; do not be discouraged, for the Lord your God will be with you wherever you go."

2. Jeremiah 17:7-8

"But blessed is the one who trusts in the Lord, whose confidence is in him. They will be like a tree planted by the water that sends out its roots by the stream. It does not fear when heat comes; its leaves are always green. It has no worries in a year of drought and never fails to bear fruit."

3. Psalm 94:19

"When anxiety was great within me, your consolation brought me joy."

4. Psalm 27:1-3

"The Lord is my light and my salvation whom shall I fear? The Lord is the stronghold of my life of whom shall I be afraid? When the wicked advance against me to devour me, it is my enemies and my foes who will stumble and fall. Though an army besiege me, my heart will not fear; though war break out against me, even then I will be confident."

5. John 14:27

"Peace I leave with you, My peace I give to you; not as the world gives do I give to you. Let not your heart be troubled, neither let it be afraid."

6. Psalm 55:22

"Cast your burden on the Lord, and He shall sustain you; He shall never permit the righteous to be moved."

7. Romans 8:31

> "What then shall we say to these things? If God is for us, who can be against us?"

8. Psalm 94:19

> "When anxiety was great within me, your consolation brought me joy."

9. Isaiah 41:10

> "So do not fear, for I am with you; do not be dismayed, for I am your God. I will strengthen you and help you; "I will uphold you with my righteous right hand.""

10. Psalm 34:4

> "I sought the Lord, and he answered me; he delivered me from all my fears.

11. Jeremiah 29:11-12

> "For I know the plans I have for you," declares the Lord, "plans to prosper you and not to harm you, plans to give you hope and a future. Then you will call on me and come and pray to me, and I will listen to you."

12. Proverbs 12:25

> "Anxiety weighs down the heart, but a kind word cheers it up."

13. Isaiah 35:4

> "Say to those with fearful hearts, "Be strong, do not fear; your God will come, he will come with vengeance; with divine retribution he will come to save you."

14. 1 John 4:18

"There is no fear in love. But perfect love drives out fear, because fear has to do with punishment. The one who fears is not made perfect in love."

15. Psalm 56:3-4

"When I am afraid, I put my trust in you. In God, whose word I praise— in God I trust and am not afraid. What can mere mortals do to me?

16. Psalm 121:1-2

"I lift up my eyes to the mountains—where does my help come from? My help comes from the Lord, the Maker of heaven and earth."

17. Hebrews 13:6

"So we say with confidence, "The Lord is my helper; I will not be afraid. What can mere mortals do to me?"

18. Hebrews 11:1

"Now faith is confidence in what we hope for and assurance about what we do not see."

19. John 14:1-2

"Do not let your hearts be troubled. You believe in God; believe also in me. My Father's house has many rooms; if that were not so, would I have told you that I am going there to prepare a place for you?"

20. Psalm 18:6

"In my distress, I called to the Lord; I cried to my God for help. From his temple, he heard my voice; my cry came before him, into his ears."

CHAPTER TEN

THE 10 BASIC NEEDS THAT WE WORRY ABOUT THE MOST

Here's a little exercise for your mind in dealing with the ten basic human needs we worry about the most. Try to fill in the blanks of what action within your power you must take to approach and deal with each need as they arise instead of worrying yourself to death and losing sleep over it.

1. The need for security and safety—I will do.......................... in order to feel safe and secure.

2. The need for companionship—I will................................ in order to find the right companion.

3. The need to live comfortably. Pay bills, put food on the table, put clothes on your body and roof over your head—I can..................................to make ends meet.

4. The need to live a healthy lifestyle—I will discipline myself in the area of..........................

5. The need to rise above every limitation and be successful in all my endeavors, dreams, goals and vision—I will challenge myself to................................

6. The need to overcome the fear of failure—I can overcome this fear by practicing daily habits of…………………………………………

7. The need to overcome self-doubt, poor selfimage and inferiority complex. I can reverse this negative perception of myself by taking the following steps………………………

8. The need to trust others and be trusted—I will ………………………………………

9. The need to be understood—I will make every effort to ………………………………

10. The need to feel respected and be valued—I will ………………………………………

Developing a strategy that helps you cope with or overcome these worries and needs gets you to a place where you are not easily or suddenly overtaken emotionally and mentally when faced or challenged by any of these needs. A strategy keeps you in check and prepares you for the worst. Approaching every need with a game plan tends to lessen the pressure and tension of trying to meet those needs. This goes back to planning. You plan your route when going on a road trip, but if you hit a detour, you adjust your strategy. It's the same with life.

One Need at a Time

Sometimes, we can get so choked up by juggling too many things simultaneously that we do nothing about the main thing that should be a priority. We can end up going in circles because we're trying to multitask. We stretch ourselves too thin.

Without a definite purpose and a plan of action, our daily task of trying to meet our needs could become cumbersome. How do you eat an elephant? One bite at a time. A day planner could be the most effective way to organize your time. This will help you prioritize the things you need attention to in their order of preference and importance.

Count the Cost

Luke 14:28-30:

> *"Suppose one of you wants to build a tower. Won't you first sit down and estimate the cost to see if you have enough money to complete it? For if you lay the foundation and are not able to finish it, everyone who sees it will ridicule you, saying, 'This person began to build and wasn't able to finish.'"*

The biblical illustration that Jesus gave in the above text shows that it pays to consider the cost or effort required to get a need met; in doing so, it might surprise you that, most times, the need will either be within your reach or out of your reach. Either way, you get a sense of direction rather than beating the air.

CHAPTER ELEVEN

GO TO BED. IT WILL BE ALL OVER IN THE MORNING

Placing your hope and trust in God instead of humans puts your mind at rest and peace…knowing that God has your back.

We are reminded in Proverbs 3:5-6 (New International Version):

"Trust in the Lord with all your heart and lean not on your own understanding; in all your ways submit to him, and he will make your paths straight."

In other words, I might get bruised on Friday and be down in the deepest valley on Saturday, but Sunday morning is coming! Your season of trial will translate to triumph in a moment if you remain steadfast and not faint. You will break free from every shackle that holds you bound. If you truly let the virtue of patience and endurance take place in your life, your worries will be all over… in the morning. You may still have the same struggles, but the worry will be gone, and you can rest assured that God has it handled.

Though 'Morning' here is a metaphor, the fact is, when you are going through the darkest moments of your life in one season, please remember that the breaking of a new day and a new season is coming.

The 23rd Book of Psalms, verse 4, gives us an insight into the comforting presence of God when we are going through our trials.

Psalm 23:4:

*"Even though I walk through the darkest valley,
I will fear no evil, for you are with me; your
rod and your staff they comfort me."*

One could tell that this 23rd Psalm, written by King David, is a psalm of desperation, perhaps of someone in despair, leaning and trusting in the everlasting arms of God for comfort and rescue from his enemies and the deep valleys of the shadow of death; he is trusting for a breakthrough from his disillusion and disorientation.

King David wrote 73 books of the Psalms, and throughout his writings, you will find in the volume of his books the writings of a man who had missed God but now desperately seeks God for restoration from his afflictions. In his plea for mercy, in the entire chapter of Psalms 51, David first poured out his heart by confessing his transgressions, flaws and shortcomings.

Psalm 51:1-3:

*"Have mercy on me, O God, according to your unfailing love;
according to your great compassion, blot out my transgressions.
Wash away all my iniquity and cleanse me from my sin. For
I know my transgressions and my sin is always before me."*

And in verse 17 of the same chapter, he acknowledges the sacrifices of God to be a broken spirit.

Psalm 51:17 (King James Version):

*"The sacrifices of God are a broken spirit: a broken and
a contrite heart, O God, thou wilt not despise."*

David lets us know in his approach toward the Creator when we sincerely come to him in our brokenness.... He's willing to heal, bind our brokenness and remove our cares and worries. Then, in Psalm 34, he brings it home.

Psalm 34:18:

> *"The Lord is close to the brokenhearted and saves those who are crushed in spirit."*

I love the way the Message Bible Translation says it differently:

Psalm 34:18 (The Message Bible Translation):

> *"If your heart is broken, you'll find God right there; if you're kicked in the gut, he'll help you catch your breath."*

Staying awake all night and worrying about the things you cannot change does not get you closer to your desired breakthrough. The more you worry, the bigger the mountain will seem to you. Your mind can magnify your problems greater than what they are in reality. Remember, what you focus on most is what grows in your life.

Here's another verse of exaltation from the psalmist:

Psalm 121:4-7:

> *"Indeed, he who watches over Israel will neither slumber nor sleep. The Lord watches over you; the Lord is your shade at your right hand; the sun will not harm you by day, nor the moon by night. The Lord will keep you from all harm...he will watch over your life."*

So the next time the enemy tries to keep you awake all night worrying and anxious over your circumstances, please remind him that the one that watches over you never sleeps nor slumbers. If God is already staying awake to watch over you, just like he watches over the sparrow, then there's no need for you to be awake, too. It won't take the two of you to watch over the night when you have him on your side. He's all you need.

One of the seven covenant Hebrew names through which God revealed himself to the Israelites is *El Shaddai*, which means the 'All sufficient one' or the 'God who is more than enough.' Therefore, because God has got you covered, it's time to go to bed and unwind in the safe hollow of his hand.

The words of our Lord and Savior Jesus, in chapter six of Saint Matthew's gospel, never fail to re-echo in my mind the moment I start worrying and experiencing sleeplessness:

Matthew 6:25-30:

> *"Therefore, I tell you, do not worry about your life, what you will eat or drink, or about your body, what you will wear. Is not life more than food and the body more than clothes? Look at the birds of the air; they do not sow or reap or store away in barns, and yet your heavenly Father feeds them. Are you not much more valuable than they? Can any one of you by worrying add a single hour to your life?*
>
> *"And why do you worry about clothes? See how the flowers of the field grow. They do not labor or spin. Yet I tell you that not even Solomon, in all his splendor, was dressed like one of these. If that is how God clothes the grass of the field, which is here today and tomorrow is thrown into the fire, will he not much more clothe you—you of little faith?"*

When you read the text further down, Jesus emphasizes how we should prioritize the kingdom of God and his righteousness, and then every other need in our lives shall be met because the Father cares and knows that we need these things.

Another resounding teaching on the mount that Jesus taught in line with our needs being met is Matthew chapter 7 from verses 7-11. I believe the heartache and disappointment we experience from our unmet needs are the root cause of our worry, anxiety and sleeplessness.

Matthew 7:7-11:

> *"Ask, and it will be given to you; seek and you will find; knock and the door will be opened to you. For everyone who asks receives; the one who seeks finds; and to the one who knocks, the door will be opened.*
>
> *"Which of you, if your son asks for bread, will give him a stone? Or if he asks for a fish, will he give him a snake? If you, then, though you are evil, know how to give good gifts to your children, how much more will your Father in heaven give good gifts to those who ask him!"*

Whenever I read the text above, I can't help but go back to the serenity prayer that I referred to earlier, written by Reinhold Niebuhr:

> "God, grant me the serenity to accept the things I cannot change, the courage to change the things I can, and the wisdom to know the difference."

I think 'the wisdom to know the difference' is where we all get stuck. Not knowing what's beyond our human power, abilities and limitations to effect a change that's desperately needed in our situation is where the challenge is. Though there's a role and a part we must all play to receive our breakthrough, we must also realize that our human nature always limits our strength and willpower…

of doubt, frailty, and the lack of insight into what the future holds. It's okay to accept your inabilities and realize that Superman is dead.

So let me leave you with this text from David, the Psalmist:

Psalm 30:5:

> *"For his anger lasts only a moment, but his favor lasts a lifetime; weeping may stay for the night, but rejoicing comes in the morning."*

And in the words of the first family of gospel music, the Winans, in collaboration with the legendary soul music diva Anita Baker:

> "Ain't no need to worry what the night is gonna bring… it will be all over in the morning."

So you can learn to trust and believe again whatever situation or circumstances life has overloaded you with, whatever the disappointment, the heartache, whatever the dreams and your hopes that have been shattered. Worrying doesn't make the journey go easier or smoother; it only puts a weight on you that slows you down. Once again, the good book admonishes us with these words:

Hebrews 12:1 (King James Version)

> *"Wherefore seeing we also are compassed about with so great a cloud of witnesses, let us lay aside every weight, and the sin which doth so easily beset us, and let us run with patience the race that is set before us."*

Worry is a weight that you ought not to carry. A songwriter says: "Come and lay down the burdens you have carried. You cannot change the situation by worrying."

SO DON'T WORRY ABOUT IT! GO TO BED

and have a good night's sleep.

CONTACT INFORMATION FOR BOOKING:

Email all requests to Pk.victoryworld@gmail.com & www.keithbanksobanor.com

@Realpkbanks — Instagram

Keith B'Banor — Facebook

@Keithbbanor — TikTok

www.ingramcontent.com/pod-product-compliance
Lightning Source LLC
Chambersburg PA
CBHW071709180426
43192CB00051B/2097